DON'T JUST
APPLAUD–
SEND MONEY!

DON'T JUST APPLAUD -
SEND MONEY!

The Most Successful Strategies for Funding and Marketing the Arts

---

ALVIN H. REISS

THEATRE COMMUNICATIONS GROUP

Reiss, Alvin H.
    Don't just applaud—send money: the most successful strategies for funding and marketing the arts / Alvin H. Reiss. — 1st ed.
    ISBN 1-55936-105-0
    1. Arts fund raising—United States—Handbooks, manuals, etc.
    I. Title
NX765.R46   1995   95-14236
700'.68'1—dc20   CIP

First Printing, October 1995
Second Printing, February 1997
Third Printing, October 2000

To James, the newest member of the Reiss family,
who has ignited in all of us a very special spark.

TABLE OF CONTENTS

CHAPTER THREE: AUDIENCE REACH

CHAPTER FOUR: SELLING TICKETS

CHAPTER FIVE: OUTRAGEOUS PROMOTIONS

CHAPTER EIGHT: FUND-RAISING EVENTS AND CONCEPTS

CHAPTER ELEVEN: THE TOURIST TRADE

Foreword

In a large sense, this book is a reflection of my activities in the arts. In fact, it might be retitled "Confessions of a Life-long Learner in the Arts," because invariably, wherever I go to lecture or consult—and my travels have taken me all over the globe—I never fail to listen, and learn, from my audiences.

What I've learned over more than thirty years of peripatetic arts involvement is that creativity is hardly limited to the cultural event or product. Working under severe financial constraints and all too often under extreme pressure, the arts field, perhaps more than any other industry, has learned to do more for less and to do it better at the same time. The more than one hundred case histories I've written for this book illustrate the resourcefulness I've discovered wherever my lectures and seminars have taken me—to large cities and small towns throughout the U.S. and Canada, and to more distant places like Nelson, New Zealand and Sydney, Australia. To heighten their significance, I've utilized a "Challenge, Plan, Result" format for each case that symbolizes another kind of "CPR"—Creativity, Persistence and Resourcefulness—that energetic administrators have given to their organizations.

I've also tried to capture another characteristic endemic to the field: a sense of humor, even in the face of funding cutbacks and other adversities. This is especially noticeable in many of the visual materials I've used to illustrate my text. Since the slides and overheads I use in my seminars have helped attendees to better experience the cases I discuss, I thought that the same technique would be useful in book form. This book, then, is almost a seminar in print and although I'm not available, as I am at my programs, to respond to questions immediately, I hope to continue the dialogue by phone or mail with many readers over the coming months and years.

Writing this book as a follow-up to my previous work for Theatre Communications Group, *Cash In! Funding and Promoting the Arts*, has been an exhausting task but most certainly a happy one. My thanks to the many arts administrators who responded to my calls (which invariably came in the middle of a funding deadline or some other momentary crisis), for information, photos and fliers and my continued admiration for their achievements. My thanks also to the dedicated professionals at Theatre Communications Group.

—Alvin H. Reiss

DON'T JUST APPLAUD–
SEND MONEY!

Chapter One

THE ARTS ARE CREATIVE

$$\overline{1}$$

USING CELEBRITIES:

Poster Pinup

CHALLENGE: With its annual one day "Operathon" fund-raiser looming on the horizon, the Lyric Opera of Chicago wanted to attract as much advance attention as possible, hoping to top the $235,000 raised the preceding year.

PLAN: In previous years, top celebrities— including Luciano Pavarotti, Placido Domingo, Governor James R. Thompson, Mayor Richard M. Daley, Ann Landers and Chicago Bears' coach Mike Ditka—posed for posters to promote the Operathon. As a topper, the opera company's director of marketing and communications, Susan Mathieson, came up with the audacious idea to "shoot the works" and approach Chicago Bulls' basketball great Michael Jordan, one of the world's highest-paid athletes. Knowing that board member Sidney L. Port was a personal friend of Bulls' broadcaster and former coach Red Kerr, she called opera company general director Ardis Krainik, who called Port, who called Kerr,

Lyric Opera of Chicago poster twins—opera company general director Ardis Krainik and basketball superstar Michael Jordan.

who called Jordan. Jordan, who earned over $30 million from endorsements that year, agreed to donate his services and pose for a picture with Ms. Krainik.

RESULT: The Jordan/Krainik photo—with the basketball star wearing a sweatshirt reading "Bullish on Lyric Opera"—was used on the cover of the Operathon program, mailed in advance to over 100,000 people. The same picture was used on billboards and posters throughout Chicago. Then the publicity deluge started. Stories and photos appeared on the AP wires, in *USA Today* and on the front page of the *Chicago Sun Times*. The Operathon raised a record $265,000, including $10,000 from posters sold for $15 each.

2

ONE WAY TO BUY A JURY:

Putting Donors Onstage

CHALLENGE: Is there a creative way to fill non-speaking roles in a drama, at the same time raising funds and promoting the production? The answer was a resounding yes for Rochester, New York's GeVa Theatre, which found a unique and lucrative way to fill ten non-speaking jury roles for a production of *Inherit the Wind*, the courtroom drama based on the famed Scopes' "Monkey Trial."

PLAN: A theatre supporter—a highly visible local corporate leader— thought this wonderful play should be sponsored by Rochester law firms. Why, he wondered, couldn't

JURY FORM
Return by December 21, 1990

_____ YES! We would like _____ jury seats.

_____ YES! We would like to buy a jury of nine.

_____ YES! We would like to buy out _____ juries of nine for a total of _____ seats.

Name: _____

Business: _____

Telephone: day _____ eve _____

Address _____
                                    (City, State, Zip)

Requested Court Day/Date/Time: 1st Choice _____
                                  2nd Choice _____
                                  3rd Choice _____

Mail Form To: Jury Duty   OR   Fax Form To:
               MRT   MRT at 324-9097
               108 East Wells Street   Attn: Mary Beth Topf
               Milwaukee, WI 53202

CONFIRMATION AND BILLING WILL BE MAILED UPON RECEIPT OF THIS FORM

INHERIT THE WIND JURY DATES

Thursday	1/10/91 8:00 pm	Tuesday	1/29/91 7:30 pm	Tuesday	2/12/91 7:30 pm
Friday	1/11/91 8:00 pm	Wednesday	1/30/91 7:30 pm	Wednesday	2/13/91 7:30 pm
Saturday	1/12/91 8:00 pm	Thursday	1/31/91 8:00 pm	Thursday	2/14/91 8:00 pm
Thursday	1/17/91 8:00 pm	Friday	2/1/91 8:00 pm	Friday	2/15/91 8:00 pm
Sunday	1/20/91 8:00 pm	Saturday	2/2/91 5:00 pm	Saturday	2/16/91 5:00 pm
		Saturday	2/2/91 9:00 pm	Saturday	2/16/91 9:00 pm
Tuesday	1/22/91 7:30 pm	Sunday	2/3/91 2:00 pm	Sunday	2/17/91 7:30 pm
Wednesday	1/23/91 7:30 pm	Sunday	2/3/91 7:30 pm		
Thursday	1/24/91 8:00 pm			Tuesday	2/19/91 7:30 pm
Friday	1/25/91 8:00 pm	Tuesday	2/5/91 7:30 pm	Wednesday	2/20/91 7:30 pm
Saturday	1/26/91 5:00 pm	Wednesday	2/6/91 7:30 pm	Thursday	2/21/91 8:00 pm
Saturday	1/26/91 9:00 pm	Thursday	2/7/91 8:00 pm	Friday	2/22/91 8:00 pm
Sunday	1/27/91 7:30 pm	Friday	2/8/91 8:00 pm	Saturday	2/23/91 8:00 pm
		Saturday	2/9/91 5:00 pm	Saturday	2/23/91 5:00 pm
		Saturday	2/9/91 9:00 pm	Sunday	2/24/91 2:00 pm
		Sunday	2/10/91 7:30 pm		

Milwaukee Repertory Theatre jury form.

they contribute $1,000 a performance and, in return, have the opportunity to fill the non-speaking jury roles with their partners and clients? With approval from the theatre, he called the heads of four law firms and won their commitment. GeVa's development director Judith Anne Stinson then wrote the remaining law firms in town inviting them to join with the other four and "buy" the jury—or ten seats on it.

RESULT: For the five weeks the show ran, GeVa sold twelve sponsorships for weekend nights to different legal and financial institutions. The neophyte actors enjoyed their theatrical debuts immensely, and the concept had strong promotional benefits as well. According to Ms. Stinson, "Every law firm used this opportunity to show off in front of all their employees, clients and friends. Every firm invited at least 200 people and had a party after the show."

Good ideas often inspire adaptation. When the Milwaukee Repertory Theatre produced *Inherit the Wind* subsequently, it went after individual "jurors" as well as firms. "Jury forms" soliciting participants for jury duty "on one of the all-time great trials"—for $100 each—were mailed. During the play's run, seventy-five served, netting the theatre $7,500.

3

SELLING SEATS—OF EVERY KIND:

Naming Opportunities for Donors

CHALLENGE: The Michigan Theater in Ann Arbor, a site listed in the National Register of Historic Places, had been saved from destruction by a group of private citizens who joined together to form a nonprofit organization to operate the landmark facility. Seven years later, the theatre was about to launch a $1.56 million renovation drive. With a half-million dollar challenge grant from a board member and additional funds already raised, the board felt a community-wide campaign with spark and drama would put the drive over the top.

PLAN: Board member and campaign chair Judy Dow-Alexander proposed adapting the traditional named-seat concept by adding other items key to the restoration but not usually offered for sale. Targeting young professionals, and using several young people as volunteers, "The Great Seat Sale" offered seats with the donor's name affixed to them forever, for $500, payable over four years. Other opportunities for naming—going as high as $250,000 for the foyer—were included in text and drawings in the restoration catalogue entitled "Buy a Piece of the Michigan." Unusual items offered included light bulbs for $10 each, signs designating "men" and "women" for $100 each and even toilets for $400 each. Described as "lavatory fixtures," the latter item was "a great gift to give to a special friend on his or her Big Four-Oh or that Fantastic

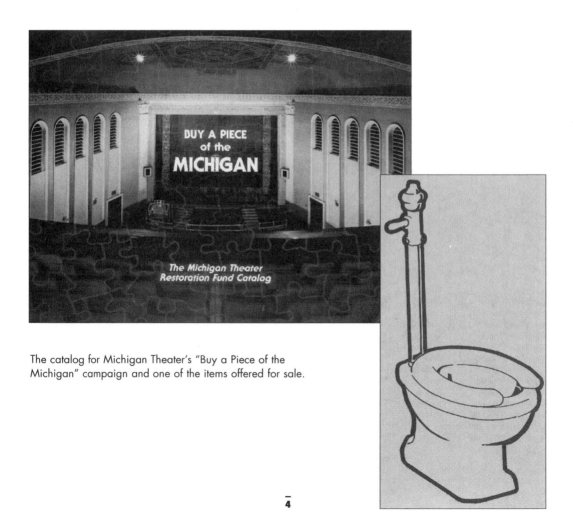

The catalog for Michigan Theater's "Buy a Piece of the Michigan" campaign and one of the items offered for sale.

Fifty. All of Michigan's friends will pause to remember your gift for years to come." Other interesting offers included the popcorn machine for $3,000 and "the perfect gift for the man who has everything": a boiler for $10,000.

RESULT: Aided by an enthusiastic "yuppie" volunteer committee—which was photographed in Roaring Twenties' garb for one brochure—and by tremendous local and national publicity—including a mention in the *Wall Street Journal*—the drive surpassed its $1.5 million goal, raising $1.8 million—including $1,200 from the sale of three toilets.

4

ARTS CENTERS HAVE THEIR UPS AND DOWNS:

Maximum Publicity from a Minor Event

CHALLENGE: While an arts center's redecorated lobby, refurbished grand staircase or even newly installed seats are worth crowing about, how do you publicize the fact that it has just installed a new elevator?

PLAN: The leaders of Spirit Square in Charlotte, North Carolina thought that the installation of a new elevator shaft, which was of practical importance to audience members, was worthy of mention. Their tactic? They made up and sold T-shirts reading "Spirit Square gets the Shaft."

RESULT: Mission accomplished. The newest addition to the Center was promoted in a tongue-in-cheek manner, and Spirit Square even made a few dollars from the sale of their T-shirts.

Flier for the Ballet Oklahoma cruise on its nautical sponsor, Holland America Line.

5

$MOOTH $AILING:

An Official Cruise Line

CHALLENGE: For a small dance company in a midwestern city, finding a corporate sponsor can be a major undertaking, and finding a national sponsor can be an even more daunting task. When Steve Vargo, a new Ballet Oklahoma board member, suggested a possible national sponsor, his idea was not only daunting but for a company in a landlocked city, totally incongruous: Vargo, a travel agent, believed the best sponsor might be a major cruise line.

PLAN: With ballet company approval, Vargo—the head of the Key to the World Travel Service—invited regional officials of the Holland America Line to attend a Ballet Oklahoma concert, where he sold them on the concept of sponsoring the dance company. His rationale was that precisely because the city was landlocked, there was a large number of ballet-company supporters who might be interested in trying sea cruises as vacations—if the cruise line were affiliated with the dance company. Through the program that was developed, the Holland America Line donated $5,000 to underwrite the next year's season-opening performance, agreed to a special "Ballet

Cruise" the following February featuring Ballet Oklahoma dancers as performers, and flew Brian Pitts, the dance company's artistic director, and his wife to Holland America headquarters in Seattle, where it videotaped them aboard the M.S. *Nieuw Amsterdam* for later viewing in Oklahoma City. On opening night, Nico van der Vorm, president of Holland America, flew to Oklahoma City, Ballet Oklahoma's home base, and met with the state's Lieutenant Governor to proclaim Holland America the official cruise line of Ballet Oklahoma. As a final boost to the campaign, which was widely publicized locally, travel agent Vargo offered exclusive advance-booking discounts to Ballet Oklahoma supporters—and donated $100 to Ballet Oklahoma for every cruise booked.

RESULT: Both parties were pleased with the results of the sponsorship. In fact, Holland America reported that the Ballet Cruise won one of its highest-ever ratings for entertainment value while attracting forty-five Ballet Oklahoma friends and dancers as passengers. The program was such a great success that it was repeated the following year with additional sponsorship fees and another Ballet Cruise. Overall, the dance company—in addition to receiving almost $20,000 from the sponsorship fees and cruise-booking donations—reaped tremendous local and national publicity and won many new friends.

Oklahoma City Philharmonic refrigerator magnets sent to subscribers to spur the return of unused tickets.

6

TICKET MAGNETISM:

Getting No-Shows to Return Unused Tickets

CHALLENGE: "No show" ticket buyers are a vexing concern for many performing-arts groups. Faced with the problem, the Oklahoma City Philharmonic set out to develop a mechanism to spur ticket-holders to return unused tickets in advance so they could be resold.

PLAN: The orchestra sent all its subscribers season listings printed on refrigerator magnets, one for the classical series and one for the pops series. Each listed guest artists and dates along with the direct message: "If you are unable to attend, please call TICKETS (842-5387) 24 hours before the concert to release your seats for a tax-deductible donation."

RESULT: During the program's first year, the orchestra had an over-fifty percent increase in the number of returned tickets. The following season, single-ticket buyers were sent magnets producing similar results on returns. Subsequently, returns increased an additional seven-and-a-half percent both for ticket holders who returned tickets for resale and for attendees as a percentage of tickets sold.

7

A RISK WORTH TAKING:

Moving to New Quarters

CHALLENGE: After ten years in the same location—just about the time its lease came due—the directors of a visual-arts space in New York City decided it was time to change and expand its program. Exit Art, as it was known then—an organization with a $400,000 annual budget—wanted to include theatre and other nighttime activities along with its visual-arts program, and its directors saw the expiring lease as both a signal and a challenge to move on. With the approval of the organization's board, they set out to find a new and expanded space—double the five thousand square feet they then had.

PLAN: Because the New York real-estate market was depressed, they were able to find a seventeen thousand square-foot space which had not been used for thirty years. Although the overall rent was higher, the per-square-footage was much more than before; and when the board saw the space and the possibilities it held, it gave the go-ahead to sign a ten-year lease. With everyone pitching in, and with co-founder Papo Colo undertaking the design work, the new space officially opened three months later—against all odds—with "Fever," an exhibition featuring the work of fifty young artists, and with a new name: Exit Art/The First World. The first stage of renovation alone—financed by board and other individual contributions, and by loans—cost $100,000.

RESULT: The arts organization quickly incorporated many of its planned concepts into its program; including Cultura, a new performance-oriented cafe, and The Apartment Store, featuring artist-made objects, with sales-income split between the organization and its artists. With a vastly expanded program and stepped-up fund-raising, the budget had grown to $600,000 and the space had reached the next stage of its development, with more renovation work ahead of it. The store was bringing in some income and the cafe was breaking even, but Exit Art/The First World still had a long way to go to realize its many objectives. According to Jeanette Ingberman, the effort was still in an experimental stage, but she, her co-director, and their board all felt it was a risk worth taking.

Chapter Two

Niche Marketing

$$\overline{1}$$

The Audience Way Up There:

Special Audience for Cheaper Seats

CHALLENGE: A marketing study for the New York City Ballet presented two key findings: 1) the largest percentage of empty seats were the least expensive ones, in the fourth ring, at the top of Lincoln Center's New York State Theater; 2) the largest group missing from the audience were people in their twenties and thirties. The ballet company recognized that—with the right kind of program—it had an opportunity to match the missing audience with the empty seats.

PLAN: The ballet company set out to develop a specific program that would not only make it affordable for young people to attend the ballet, but would also make the experience as exciting as possible, in a warm, social environment among others new to the dance. Focusing specifically on the empty seats, the new "Fourth Ring Society" offered special benefits to the target audience: membership at $10 a season, with the opportunity to buy fourth-ring tickets for only $10 each; pre-performance lectures; free cappuccino at intermission; restaurant discounts; a free New York City Ballet T-shirt; and a souvenir book. Using rented mailing lists fitting the demographic profile—with an emphasis on credit-card holders—the ballet company mailed one hundred thousand brochures prior to the start of the fall season, and backed up the mailing with print and radio ads. Lighthearted ads about the "new alternative for people on the way up" emphasized the fun of belonging, of meeting people and doing things "you couldn't do in Kansas."

RESULT: In its first year, the Society had 1,709 members and sold 4,062 tickets, figures that rose to 2,244 members and 9,130 tickets sold during the second year. Later, with the only change in the program an increased membership fee of $15, results went down slightly; but, according to Elizabeth Healy, the ballet company's director of press and promotion, that was probably a positive development, since many Society members converted to regular subscribers or purchased single tickets at higher prices.

IT'S BACK.
NEW YORK CITY BALLET'S FOURTH RING SOCIETY.
$10 TAKES YOU RIGHT TO THE TOP.

The Fourth Ring Society is a special way to be part of New York, *and* to see extraordinary ballet. It's a club—with some truly unique benefits: Great seats for the world's most exciting ballet company. Special discounts. Behind-the-scenes glimpses. A chance to meet other questing young New Yorkers. And all for an entry fee of just $10 a year—less than *one* movie ticket, with a bag of popcorn!

SO MUCH FOR SO LITTLE.

A free NYCB t-shirt. Fourth Ring tickets for just $10 each to New York City Ballet's Winter and Spring repertory seasons. And, you can bring a friend for just $10 more. Free access to special NYCB "First Positions" discussions. "Fourth Ring" discounts to some of the hottest area restaurants. Coupon for free cappuccino at our Fourth Ring Cappuccino Bar. "Season Updates"—with the latest schedules, news and gossip. A personal ID card and number that makes things happen faster. Your own copy of the 1992 commemorative Gala Souvenir Book.

JOINING THE FOURTH RING SOCIETY IS A SIMPLE WAY TO GET IN ON THE BEST THIS CITY HAS TO OFFER.

You're always saying there's no place "different" and "exciting" to go. You're always wondering what other people are doing for fun. Well, here's a deal that gives you all that, *and* won't demolish your paycheck. So, go ahead—the gym will still be there tomorrow. Take a chance on something that stretches your soul. After all, isn't that why you're living here?

The New York City Ballet's Fourth Ring Society membership brochure.

2

REACHING THE UNREACHED:

New Approach to People of Color

CHALLENGE: The Lincoln Center Theater was pleased with the tremendous success of its membership program, an alternative to the traditional subscription concept. The program allows members paying an annual fee—now $25—to purchase tickets for any theatre production for only $15 a play and $20 a musical, up from the $10 a show that was charged when the concept was originally adopted. However, the theatre found its efforts to recruit younger, less affluent theatregoers and people of color to its audience was thwarted because the $25 annual membership fee proved a deterrent.

PLAN: Following a focus-group study, which confirmed that price was a key barrier, the theatre waived its $25 fee for the targeted audience for the first year. A low-key recruitment campaign, deliberately avoiding any announcement in the general press, was launched through an ad in a black-oriented arts magazine, *Black Masks*, and through leaflets and program inserts distributed at a Kwanza festival, at other events of interest to the target group and through mailings to people who used "two-fer" coupons to see Lincoln Center Theater productions with themes or settings of interest to black audiences. Prospective members learned that they could activate "free memberships" with their first low-price tickets order. Boosted by word of mouth, the campaign was so successful that a planned advertising and direct mail follow-up was never undertaken.

RESULT: The response was tremendous, with 13,842 new members enrolled. In fact, because of the success, the theatre had to suspend its offer by the end of the season. Survey results were revealing and heartening: new members were much younger and had much lower incomes than regular members, and over fifty-six percent of those surveyed indicated that they attended the theatre only "every now and then" or "never." A little more than half were single and forty-four percent were African-Americans, compared to only three percent of regular members. Although only twenty-four percent bought additional tickets, the theatre was pleased with the renewal results, which showed that 3,925 members, or more than twenty-eight percent, renewed for the next season as fee-paying members.

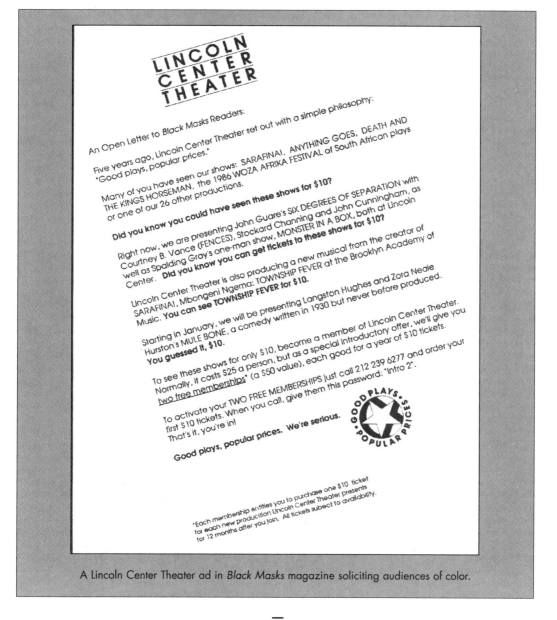

A Lincoln Center Theater ad in *Black Masks* magazine soliciting audiences of color.

—
3
—

NO LANGUAGE BARRIER:

Approaching Potential Audience on its Terms

CHALLENGE: Vancouver has a large Chinese-Canadian community that the Vancouver Opera hoped to involve in its program. However, since the potential audience was largely unfamiliar with Western opera and the company's work, the Opera knew that any audience-development initiative would have to be an intensive, long-term effort, based on a cooperative partnership. Immediate results, it reasoned, were less important than its commitment to an ongoing relationship.

PLAN: Recognizing the need for professional marketing expertise, the Opera enlisted the consultant services of an advertising and public relations agency—Scali, McCabe, Sloves—experienced in working with the Chinese community. A full plan was developed one summer with Chinese-Canadian board member Sophia Leung playing a key role. In the fall, the opera company submitted a proposal to Vancouver's Office of Cultural Affairs for a $7,200 grant to fund the project. When the grant was denied, the Opera, committed to the concept, found the funds from its own budget. Key to the partnership was a concept which the opera company termed "an educational relationship-building focus rather than a self-serving sales focus."

Aimed at a target group of immigrants to Vancouver who had arrived within the preceding five years, aged fifteen and older, with average skills in English and receptivity to western culture, the program included as key elements: development of an ongoing relationship with Chinese media through such efforts as backstage tours, information luncheons, performances and joint promotional opportunities; a regular opera column in the Chinese-language *Sing Tao Daily*, including articles on Western opera history, Chinese personalities in opera, and how new audience members might prepare to attend opera performances; and publicity initiatives such as magazine features and Chinese-language public-service announcements. The opera company also planned a board staff cultural-diversity workshop, open to other city arts groups, and an ongoing program of involvement with leaders of the Chinese-Canadian community through establishment of an advisory council.

RESULT: By the end of its first year, the program was considered to have met its preliminary goals. Accomplishments included successful projects aimed at the Chinese media, opera participation in Chinese-Canadian events, positive reception of the ongoing newspaper column, and the appearance of articles in Chinese-language publications. Although Vancouver Opera initially paid for space in Chinese publications, in time their material was deemed newsworthy, and they received a good deal of free editorial space in the following months. While there was no dramatic increase in attendance by the target audience, inroads were made. With the program geared to long-term development, the opera company was pleased with its progress.

4

THE CARIBBEAN WAY:

Reaching the Right Audience

CHALLENGE: The Lincoln Center Theater production of *Playboy of the West Indies*, a Caribbean version of *Playboy of the Western World*, was oriented, in setting and theme, toward New York's large Caribbean-American and African-American communities. The target audience, however, was not a significant part of the theatre's constituency and could not be reached through its usual marketing techniques.

PLAN: The theatre developed a marketing plan based on discounted tickets, promoting them through "two-fer" offers, group sales and—importantly—ads in community newspapers that served the target market.

Lincoln Center Theater discount ticket offer.

RESULT: About one-third of all tickets for the production—over 9,000—were sold to people of color—a remarkable achievement.

5̄

A SINGULAR CONCERN:

Marketing to Singles

CHALLENGE: If arts group put out "most wanted" posters for audiences, many would feature singles. With years of event-attending ahead of them, disposable dollars in their wallets and purses, and with an acknowledged susceptibility to the lure of upbeat social activities involving other singles, they are highly sought. The Roundabout Theatre Company in New York City, as eager to reach this audience as any of its artistic counterparts, set out to develop an approach that would be on-target and expansive, building over the years so that singles would become a large and significant audience segment. Besides, thought Roundabout's general manager, Ellen Richard, it would be a good way for the singles on her staff to find dates.

PLAN: Roundabout adopted a tongue-in-cheek approach to introduce its first "Single Series"—five plays followed by complimentary cocktail receptions, with liquor provided courtesy of Johnny Walker. Fliers and ads referred to the series as "the antidote to singles bars and blind dates with your mother's friend's cousin with a 'great personality.'" Ads in "personals" sections began "Theatre, 26, looking for singles to share dramatic evenings on Broadway." Boosted by a tremendous response, with the initial singles series turning into *five* singles series during the program's season, Roundabout moved into new but related territory with a "Gay & Lesbian Singles Series," promoted in one local news-weekly in the "Men Seeking Men" section as "an inspired antidote to the bar scene." Pleased with the program's success, Schefflin & Somerset, which represented Johnny Walker, decided to switch sponsorship brands to Dewar's, because that brand's ad campaign was geared towards a young, single audience. Since the initial campaign, Roundabout has maintained its light on-target touch in fliers and ads, including one headlined "Unfortunately...Anita

Bryant, Pat Robertson, Ronald Reagan, Jimmy Swaggart, Cardinal O'Connor, Sam Nunn, Rush Limbaugh and Jesse Helms are unable to attend Roundabout Theatre Company's Gay & Lesbian Singles Evening...but perhaps you can."

RESULT: Within three seasons, Roundabout's Dewar's Single Series had grown into nine separate series with 3,300 subscribers. In addition to drawing new audiences, the series also won increased press attention, highlighted by a *New York Times* photo and caption in its widely read "On Stage, and Off" section showing a Roundabout first: a photo of an engaged couple who met at a Single Series performance.

6

APPEALING TO THE GAY COMMUNITY:

Co-sponsor Helps Open Doors

CHALLENGE: Recognizing that there was a significant number of gay people in its community, the Austin (Texas) Lyric Opera decided to develop a marketing program aimed at this special audience.

PLAN: The opera company invited the *Texas Triangle*, a statewide gay and lesbian weekly, to join it as sponsor of a promotion linking performance attendance with an onstage reception and tour. Boosted by free advertising and editorial space in the *Triangle*, the "Triangle on Stage" (TOS) promotion drew a large enough audience at the company's season-ending performance to justify a full-scale promotional effort the following season. That summer, a ten-member volunteer steering committee of gay men and lesbians was organized to help develop three social events to take place prior to opera performances, and to coordinate promotional plans.

The campaign kicked off on Labor Day weekend, to coincide with Pride Week, which involved thousands of Austin gays and lesbians. It also marked the start of the *Triangle's* promotional blitz, which included full-page ads on the campaign and the opera-company season, a feature story on Triangle on Stage and interviews with the Opera's general director and TOS chair. During the rest of September, additional exposure came from three full-page *Triangle* ads and from booths set up at Pride Week sites, two upscale gay and lesbian bookstores and a film festival aimed at the gay community.

RESULT: Utilizing a prospect list of 309 names generated by the promotion, the committee issued invitations to each of the three events—a reception with door prizes, held at the home of a gay Opera board member; a backstage tour prior to a *Marriage of Figaro* performance; and a reception for attendees at a national conference on gay and lesbian studies held at the nearby University of Texas. By season's end, the opera company had won over fifty new subscribers and well over one hundred single-ticket buyers. "While the response was not overwhelming," said Revah Anzaldua, the Opera's director of marketing and public relations who conceived of the campaign, "both partners in the effort agree that the partnership served a much greater goal for all involved. Austin Lyric Opera generated an enormous amount of good will and positive press at little or no cost and has built a bridge into the gay and lesbian community. The *Texas Triangle* has gained an example of effective target-marketing that it can offer to other 'straight' businesses and has enhanced the marketability of its young newspaper." The Opera board viewed the program as so significant that it made it a regular component of its Community Program Committee.

7

PLAYING TAG:

Getting Young Audiences to Carry Your Message

CHALLENGE: Children are a key audience for the Crossroads Arts Council in Rutland, Vermont, with Council educational programs in local schools reaching about 10,000 county youngsters each year. The Council, whose marketing committee was interested in developing new audiences in the twenty-five to forty year-old age-range, wanted to turn the childrens' enthusiasm into a positive force that would be helpful in spurring their parents to become arts attendees and supporters.

PLAN: The Council told every school where it booked a performance, workshop or residency that it would provide stickers for all the children to wear home at the end of the day. The bright red stickers read, "Ask me about the Crossroads performance today..."

RESULT: The kids enjoy wearing the tags and, according to council director Vicky Young, they take their enthusiasm home. While it's been difficult to quantify the program's effectiveness, Ms. Young believes that it's "worthwhile, inexpensive and simple to implement, and results in awareness about the organization, if not increased ticket sales."

Tags given to schoolchildren to wear by the Crossroads Arts Council.

Chapter Three

Audience Reach

1

THE BARGAIN TICKET:

Audiences Pay What They Can

CHALLENGE: The San Diego Theatre League was seeking an inexpensive way to make the general public more aware of its half-price ticket booth, Times Arts Tix. The four-year-old booth needed some dynamic event to recapture the hoopla that had surrounded both its opening and its relocation to its permanent site. Also, while attacks on the National Endowment for the Arts were increasing and local public funding was in jeopardy, the League wanted to make a strong positive statement on behalf of the arts.

PLAN: Seeking to attract media attention, draw large crowds and promote arts attendance, the League introduced a "Bargain Arts Day" at its booth. While the "pay what you can concept" has been used by many individual theatres in the past, the League's Day was, to its knowledge, the first that involved an entire arts community offering thousands of tickets. Trumpeted as its "Gift to the City," the League promoted the event with color flyers distributed throughout the year, with no purchase-offer refused. On event day, a stage featuring entertainment by participating theatres was set up and balloons were handed out.

RESULT: The first Bargain Arts Day far exceeded League expectations, with lines stretching four blocks and tremendous media response. In seven hours, the two ticket windows were able to sell all they could handle—1,975 tickets at an average price of $1.16 each. Although intended as a one-time effort, the event's success caused the League to seek and find a corporate sponsor—Wells Fargo, which had recently purchased a hometown bank—to underwrite the next year's event, cover League staff expenses and provide the booth with necessary general-operating funds. Bargain Arts Day has become an annual event, providing what League executive director Alan Ziter calls "a pre-summer-season promotion boost for the Times Arts Tix booth on television, radio and in print media that we could never afford to buy. Patrons have come to ask about Bargain Arts Day all year round and the feedback we get from customers is phenomenal."

Over the years advance promotion has increased, with catalogs of available performances distributed a week prior to the event. Also, the ticket sales operation has been streamlined, with some 4,000 tickets a year now sold—although promotion, rather than income, is still the prime benefit. (The League now encourages people to "pay what they can afford," as opposed to "what they can," but the average price paid per ticket has increased only slightly, to about $1.40.) According to Ziter, both careful organization and entertainment play prominent roles in the event's success. "Although the lines are long," he added "patrons are kept informed and moving and a giant showboard displays sold-out performances to minimize disappointment." Patrons are also kept happy with promotional giveaways, food and drink from area restaurants made available, and stage events which not only make the wait bearable but allow theatres to showcase current productions and those that will open soon.

Audiences watching a performer at the San Diego Theater League's Bargain Arts Day.

$$\overline{\underline{2}}$$

A Taste of Theatre:

Sample Series Links Theatres

CHALLENGE: With twenty member-theatres throughout the state of New Jersey, many in close proximity to each other, the New Jersey Theatre Group sought a promotional concept that would not only boost attendance at each of the theatres but would encourage theatregoers to visit theatres they had never before attended. The Group recognized that the key to a successful program was flexibility, seat availability and low ticket prices.

PLAN: With the enthusiastic endorsement of its member companies, the NJTG introduced a trial "Theatre Sampler Series" that promised patrons "three shows, your choice, three dates, your choice, and three theatres, your choice, for the choice price of $55." To keep costs down, NJTG mailed to a sample of only 500 names from around the state, selected from its mailing list of 20,000. Fliers included information on the program and the upcoming productions scheduled for each of the theatres, a map pinpointing the location of each theatre, and order forms instructing ticket buyers to list one production at each of three different theatres and to return the forms with their checks for $55, plus $3 handling, to the New Jersey Theatre Group. Purchasers were told they did not have to specify dates, since by return mail they would receive vouchers for the theatres and productions they listed, redeemable by mail or in person, with a choice of two dates.

RESULT: The returns on the first mailing exceeded expectations, with 75 orders received—a 15% response. Buoyed by the results, the Theatre Group was able to get the Geraldine Dodge Foundation to fund an August mailing for the fall season to the entire list of 20,000 names, supplemented by lists provided by some of the member-theatres of their single-ticket buyers who traveled thirty miles or more to attend a performance. While the returns weren't anywhere near that of the initial mailing, with 180 orders placed, they were still positive enough for the NJTG to make the Sampler Series a permanent addition to its program. The Sampler flier served a second purpose—as a calendar for all the theatres—and the program has also brought feedback from its participants. The Theatre Group sent survey forms to the 255 theatregoers who "sampled" the first year, and *all* 255 returned the forms, with 85% indicating that they had gone to theatres they had never before attended. According to executive director Laura Aden, dozens of people have since called the Theatre Group to commend them, and since the same comment was voiced over and over again, the comment was added to the cover of the next Theatre Sampler Series brochure: "What a Great Idea!"

3

PASS OR FAIL:

One Pass for Many Arts Groups

CHALLENGE: The Aspen/Snowmass Council for the Arts in Colorado, while looking for ways to fulfill a primary mission—to increase and improve access to the arts for residents and visitors—also was searching to find new ways of raising funds to support its own activities. The task wasn't easy. Because the Council is a service agency—with twenty-four local member arts organizations—rather than a presenter and programmer, it can't earn money through ticket sales or class fees and must look to other concepts with its overall mission.

PLAN: With the active support of its member groups, the Council introduced the "Amazing Arts Pass" to accomplish two key aims—to boost attendance at local arts events and bring in needed income for the Council. Through the program, the Council sells two passes: one for $35 and a second for $50. While both passes allow free admission to one event at each of the twelve member groups on a space-available basis, $50 donors receive *two* passes and an additional bonus: 10% off one purchase at each of eight local art galleries. Tickets are made available by participating groups on performance days, either early in the day or just before performance time. Passes are promoted through mailings to the Council list of 2,600 names, through 6,000 local bank inserts, through press notices, and through bus cards, flyers and a twelve-foot banner hung above Main Street. Local radio station KSPN-FM gives the

The 1994

Amazing Arts Pass

Presented by:

Aspen/Snowmass
Council for the Arts

Passholder   *(Non-transferable)*
Good for ONE FREE ADMISSION to one event
of each arts organization on a space-available basis.
Restrictions listed on the reverse side.

☐   **Anderson Ranch Arts Center**
☐   **Aspen Art Museum**
☐   **Aspen Dance Connection**
☐   **Aspen Filmfest**
☐   **Aspen Historical Society**
☐   **Aspen Writers' Foundation**
☐   **DanceAspen**
☐   **Aspen Music Festival**
☐   **Aspen Stage**
☐   **Aspen Theatre in the Park**
☐   **Jazz Aspen at Snowmass**   283
☐   **Wheeler Associates**

The Aspen/Snowmass Council for the Arts and
present:

The **Amazing Arts Pass**

PARTICIPATING ORGANIZATIONS

Anderson Ranch Arts Center
Aspen Art Museum
Aspen Dance Connection
Aspen Filmfest
Aspen Historical Society
Aspen Writers' Foundation
DanceAspen
Aspen Music Festival
Aspen Theatre in the Park
Jazz Aspen at Snowmass
Wheeler Associates

It IS Amazing! One FREE ticket* to the Aspen Music Festival concert of your choice, one free ticket to DanceAspen, one free ticket to an Aspen Writers' Conference reading, one free ticket to an Aspen Theatre in the Park performance, one free admission to the Aspen Art Museum—the list goes on.

That's the AMAZING ARTS PASS. It is yours for a $35 donation to the Arts Council. For a contribution of $50 or more you'll receive 10% off at participating galleries.

The AMAZING ARTS PASS is available NOW at the Wheeler Box Office, 920-5770.

* Some restrictions apply. Tickets are on a space-available basis; most organizations release tickets on the day of performance. Pass NOT good for special events, benefits, operas or Sunday concerts at the Aspen Music Festival or for opening nights of a show or company at DanceAspen or Aspen Theatre in the Park, Writers' Conference offers a lecture, reading OR film screening in June.

Aspen/Snowmass Council for the Arts • P O Box 4615 • Aspen, CO 81612

PARTICIPATING GALLERIES

Anderson Ranch Gallery
Aspen Art Museum
David Floria Gallery
Huntsman Gallery of
   Fine Art, Ltd.
Squash Blossom Gallery
The Basalt Gallery
The Omnibus Gallery
The Upper Edge Gallery

The Aspen/Snowmass Council for the Arts' Amazing Arts Pass.

promotion a major boost through its donation of $1,500 worth of air time in exchange for its identification as the program's sole media sponsor. In addition to direct mail, passes are sold at the largest box office in the community, the Wheeler Opera House.

RESULT: The Amazing Arts Pass has met its goals since its inception, attracting new audiences and new money. Member groups have been pleased with the influx of new attendees, and the Council has also been pleased with the financial results, since the number of Pass buyers and the amount of money raised has increased each year. About 200 passes were sold—for $8,000—during the program's first year, with the figure doubling to about 400 sold and $16,000 raised the next year. Now an ongoing, established success, the pass program raises about $20,000 a year for the Council from the sale of approximately 500 passes—a somewhat "amazing" result.

4

A COMIC APPROACH:

Comic Book Sells Opera

CHALLENGE: The Arizona Opera, building towards a major festival presentation of Wagner's entire four-opera Ring Cycle, faced a challenge not unknown to opera companies over the years: how to educate audiences and familiarize them with Wagner's monumental work in advance, in order to create excitement for the festival.

PLAN: Presenting a different Ring opera each year as part of the regular season, the opera company reasoned that a Wagner audience could be developed among the company's regular audience. Still, they felt something more could be done to involve non-Wagnerians in a non-threatening way. The idea they came up with was a "comical" one, emphasizing fun and whimsy: while producing *Die Walküre*, the Opera bought copies of DC Comics' *The Ring of the Nibelung* and offered them for sale to ticket buyers. The full-color comic book version presents the entire tetralogy in easy-to-follow form.

A page from DC Comics' *The Ring of the Nibelung* used to promote the Arizona Opera's Ring Cycle.

RESULT: The comic books have been very successful, with the Opera receiving income—a portion of the price of each book goes to the company as a donation—as well as "Wagnerizing" its audiences. The first shipment sold out within a month and in the end 600 copies were sold. According to marketing/PR director Laura Schairer, the comic book also helped to "dramatically increase awareness of the festival, with a survey showing that about 65% of the respondents were planning to attend."

5

A *COMFORTING THOUGHT:*

Casual Dress Day Funds Arts

CHALLENGE: Davina Grace Hill, executive director of the Salisbury-Wicomico Arts Council in Salisbury, Maryland, was thinking about a slight but peevish problem on a very hot summer day. Why, she wondered as she sat in her un-air-conditioned office, are otherwise rational people forced to wear suits and ties or hose and heels to work during the muggiest days of summer? As an arts administrator always looking for ways to turn sticky situations into fund-raising opportunities, she conceived an answer that, at least for one day, could make people in her local community be comfortably dressed and, at the same time, put needed dollars into her organization's coffers.

PLAN: The plan she devised was the first "Arts and Comfort Day," a day on which local companies allow their employees to wear casual clothes to work—*if* they donate $1 to the Arts Council. After winning the support of top local government officials, she took the mayoral proclamation she had received to area companies, asking them to endorse the idea. She also asked them to designate an employee to collect and mail contributions to the Arts Council, and to distribute to all buyers a button with a slogan above the Arts Council logo: "I'm Comfortable with the Arts." A key argument in her soft-sell to local businesses was the promise that it wouldn't cost them anything and that the total time committed by the designated employee would probably not exceed half an hour.

RESULT: The first Arts and Comfort Day was a rousing success—especially for a community with a population of only 17,000 people. Tied in to a Council-sponsored free performance of *Twelfth Night* in the park that evening, the event had participation from more then 2,000 employees from sixty local companies. While giving a promotional boost to an Arts Council that demonstrated that it was neither elitist nor stuffy, the Day also spurred company morale, with spontaneous contests launched to see who wore the most comfortable outfit to work and a number of informal company "Comfort Day" picnics erupting. In addition to the $1 donations, there were other unexpected financial rewards as some companies thanked the Arts Council by matching their employees' contributions. One company—which didn't participate and had never funded the Council—sent a check on behalf of each of its hundreds of employees.

Since the beginning, the now-annual event has grown not only in Salisbury (where the fee has increased to $2, company participation has doubled, and $3,100 was raised in a recent year) but throughout the country, where other arts groups and nonprofits have adopted the idea. Now using "I'm casually suited for the arts" stickers designed by local artist Erick Sahler instead of buttons, the event is also tied in to an end-of-day happy hour at a local club, with all sticker-wearers admitted without charge. "Perhaps the major benefit, aside from the money," said Ms. Hill, "is that our entire community is now comfortable with the arts."

6

CHILD CARE:

Baby-sitting Service for Audience

CHALLENGE: Perhaps the market wasn't a giant one, but it was worth tapping. The market in question was the parents of young children, who, staff members of the American Repertory Theatre in Cambridge, Massachusetts reasoned, might be interested in attending performances if they had someone to watch their youngsters.

PLAN: The idea of introducing an A.R.T. "Child-Care Series" allowing parents to attend matinee performances while their children participated in supervised educational and play activities, came out of a staff marketing meeting. The plan—introduced in subscription mailings—was simple: at a cost of $10 a child per performance, subscribers could leave youngsters, aged two to ten, with qualified daycare workers, including several theatre staffers, in a nearby Radcliffe College building; drop-offs could be made prior to the 2:00 pm curtain—as early as 12:15 pm if parents wished to attend pre-performance discussions—and children could be picked up after the show.

RESULT: The program worked well enough during its first season to become an ongoing special series. During the second year, seventeen children from twelve households (twenty-four subscriptions) participated in the five-day series, and seven children from five households (ten subscriptions) participated in the three-day play series. Some single-ticket buyers also took advantage of the program. An average of twenty children per performance were supervised by three staff members. Participating parents were delighted by the program's availability.

7

Thought for Food:

Free Dinners Lure Single-ticket Buyers

CHALLENGE: When a season reaches the midway point with tickets still available for the remaining productions, most performing-arts groups look for ways to woo single-ticket and mini-subscription series buyers. The stakes are high. Not only are there unsold seats to be sold, but the very real possibility exists of converting satisfied ticket buyers into next season's subscribers. Facing this situation some years ago, and aware that price-sensitive audiences might be won with extra benefits, Buffalo's Studio Arena Theatre hoped to develop an approach that could utilize its primary selling tool— telemarketing—to attract ticket buyers.

PLAN: The theatre added a new feature to its ticket campaign: A week after potential buyers had been called but still had not purchased tickets, theatre telemarketers called back with a special offer—a free dinner certificate for two at a local restaurant for every two tickets purchased. The offer was made possible thanks to local restaurants which contributed the certificates in return for program recognition or complimentary tickets.

RESULT: During the program's second season, 437 voucher packages (passes to be redeemed in return for tickets) worth $45,818 were sold. Also 1,638 "mini-packages" (tickets with date and seat) worth $111,611 were sold. Due to the campaign's success, the theatre continues to offer similar programs.

Chapter Four

Selling Tickets

1

SURPRISE REPRISE:

Making Art Less Intimidating

CHALLENGE: When a high percentage of the potential audience thinks an art form is too formal or even intimidating, it's time to try to change that perception with a lively, upbeat promotion. That's what the Indianapolis Opera did when its public relations agency, Hickman + Associates (subsequently renamed KDH Communications) came up with a humorous print and television-spot campaign built around a heroine of Wagnerian proportions and a theme: "It's all over for the fat lady." With a subscription increase of nearly 40%, the agency and the opera company wondered if they could do something a little different, but equally effective, the following season.

PLAN: The agency turned to parody, producing a subscription brochure modeled after a well-known tabloid. With giant letters at the top of the newspaper-styled brochure announcing "Exposé," the *Indianapolis Opera Inquirer*'s screaming headlines touted such stories as "Shocking Secrets Revealed: Show Salesman By Day, Opera Fan by Night" and "Doctors Say Ordering Opera Tickets Conquers Depression." Featured inside were such titillating items as "Husband Says: Opera Saved Our Marriage" and "Jeanne Nixon (sic) Predicts Tragedy, Suffering For All Who Fail to Get Season Tickets." The centerfold, headed "New Season Outrageous," provided details on upcoming productions and subscription order forms.

RESULT: Lightning struck twice. The reaction of the community was instant and positive. Tickets sales went up again—by 33%.

2

SELLING SUBSCRIPTIONS IS MURDER:

Eye-Catching Brochure

CHALLENGE: The New Orleans Opera wanted its season to be noticed. It felt it needed a departure from its traditional subscription brochure to arouse the interest of the local community and make opera seem more accessible and less intimidating.

PLAN: Stealing a leaf from the shocking tactics used by other opera companies to announce their seasons, the company published 70,000 copies of the *New Orleans Opera News*. Modeled after a supermarket tabloid, the newspaper/subscription brochure featured a front page screaming out such everyday opera themes as "Vendetta!...Murder!...Chicanery!...Passion!" and a piercing knife showing how operas "go straight to the heart." The inside pages described each of the season's four operas as if they were newspaper stories in periodicals of the time, including the 1699 *Highlands Investigator* article headlined "Murder on the Moor!" about *Lucia di Lammermoor* and the 1393 *Verona Democrat* shocker, "Suicide Pact Dooms Teenage Couple," describing *Romeo et Juliette*.

RESULT: According to Dean M. Shapiro, the opera company's director of media and publicity, the tabloid "certainly made people sit up and take notice of us." The opera company received calls and letters congratulating them on their approach, along with considerable media coverage including a feature in the *Chicago Tribune*. It also won third place in the New Orleans Press Club's annual "Best Publication" contest. Importantly, while subscription sales were declining for other local groups, New Orleans Opera subscription held steady at about 3,000, a figure close to capacity.

Vendetta! ... Murder! ...
Chicanery! ... Passion!!

NEW ORLEANS

OPERA NEWS

Volume 50   1993 – 1994

Operas arouse excitement...

and go straight to the heart!!!

New Orleans Opera Marks 50th Year

Subscribe Now

SEASON SUBSCRIPTION

HUGE SAVINGS
on Student, Group Rates

and catch the action
as 9 die onstage!

Family vendettas, brutal murders, unbridled passion, divine miracles and turnabout as fair play! Excitement reigns as the New Orleans Opera Association celebrates its "Jubilee in '93!"

Subscriptions are on sale for what promises to be one of the most exciting seasons in the company's fifty year history. Sparked by a power-packed slate of three tragedies and one comedy, opera officials are confidently predicting record sales when the season opens in October.

Subscriptions are going fast! With renewals already at their highest levels ever, the remaining seats will go to those who order as early as possible. Now is the time to order. Call or write, but don't delay.

Subscriber benefits include as much as 25% savings over single ticket prices.

Students of all ages should take advantage of the special **Student Discount** $30.00 off any season subscription price. Students may attend four operas for as little as $50.00.

Group rates are also available. "We're going to sell every seat in the house to subscribers this year", said General Director Arthur Cosenza.

Don't miss the action! Don't miss the passion! **DON'T DELAY!** Call today (504) 529-2278 and

Subscribe Now

The cover of the New Orleans Opera's subscription brochure.

3

CHILD LABOR—OF LOVE:

Children as Subscription Sales Force

CHALLENGE: If Girl Scouts are good at selling cookies, why couldn't other youngsters be equally successful selling symphony orchestra tickets—if they had the right incentive? That reasoning prompted the Oklahoma City Philharmonic to see if schoolchildren might be a key sales force for the orchestra's annual Family Series. Perhaps with the aid of youngsters, the Family Series—which had attracted only 400 subscribers the previous year—might realize its goal: to make tickets available to the largest possible audience at the lowest possible price. Since outside funding paid for most of the Family Series, filling seats was a greater concern than making money.

PLAN: Prior to the start of its season, the orchestra—with the approval of the central administration for three school systems and thirteen private schools—introduced the Family Series Fling Sales Event into sixty-one schools—fifty-eight at the elementary and middle-school level and three at the high school level. The program was designed with incentives for both participating schools and for the student sales force, depending on the number of tickets sold during a two-week period in September, shortly after the school year started. The orchestra agreed to donate $5 for each subscription sold in a participating school to that school's music program. In addition, the top-selling elementary-level class in each school was to be awarded a pizza party contributed by local restaurants and each participating student in the top-selling secondary-level class was to be given two free tickets to a regular orchestra concert. The city's top individual student ticket seller would be awarded a trip for two to Sea World in San Antonio, Texas, while every student who sold at least one Family Series Ticket was to receive a complimentary Family Series season ticket. Sales packets, which included subscription brochures for the three-concert series, order forms and confirmation notices, were distributed in advance to all participating classes.

RESULT: The orchestra was ecstatic over the results. The more than 4,500 youngsters involved in the incentive program helped boost Family Series subscriptions to over 1,500, with more than 1,100 sold by the youngsters. Overall, in dollar terms, Family Series ticket sales went up from $7,661 to $18,840, with net income nearly $10,000.

A sales packet for the Oklahoma City Philharmonic's Family Series.

4

A SPECIAL DELIVERY:

Home Delivery of Theatre Tickets

CHALLENGE: It's become easy to pick up tickets for arts events. While mail sales are commonplace, tickets can also be picked up at the box office prior to curtain time, at ticket service sites, at retail outlets and, in many cities, at half-price or other discount ticket booths. But how many people get their tickets personally delivered to their door by a courier in formal dress? Noticing how popular home deliveries of other items were, Carnegie Mellon Drama in Pittsburgh wondered if there was a market for home delivery of its theatre tickets.

PLAN: Viewing the market for a home-delivery ticket system as minor, the theatre nonetheless thought that the added service would be worth testing if deliveries could be made easily, inexpensively and, perhaps, elegantly. The theatre soon reached an agreement with a food-delivery service, Wheel Deliver, to place a $180 ad in the services' quarterly brochure announcing the ticket-delivery program. Under the arrangement, anyone calling the theatre box office and wishing home delivery of tickets could have their order charged to a credit card, with $3.25 or $4.25 added for delivery, depending on location. Tickets would be delivered, on the date the purchaser selected, by a tuxedo-clad delivery person.

RESULT: The theatre had only limited home-delivery sales during its first season, including a number to handicapped people. However, it reaped a fair amount of press coverage. Recognizing that home-delivery wasn't cost effective for most potential ticket buyers and that its greatest appeal would be for special occasions, the theatre decided to target the offer to people interested in having tickets delivered as a personalized gift or surprise item to commemorate some event or date. During its second season, the theatre's ad in the Wheel Deliver brochure suggested tickets as romantic Valentine's Day gifts. The response was immediate and—if not overwhelming—still significant enough for the theatre to continue on a targeted basis, especially considering the program's minimal cost of operation.

5

SCREEN TEST:

Movies Provide Season Themes for Opera

CHALLENGE: Despite favorable reviews of its programs, the Cincinnati Opera was selling only 54% of the house. Recognizing that many potential operagoers viewed opera as an elitist art form, the opera staff decided that it had to strip away its somber image and promote opera as fun, relevant, accessible and romantic.

PLAN: Needing a populist approach, the opera's then-new marketing director, Patricia K. Beggs, hit upon the idea of relating the company's entire promotional effort to popular entertainment and current events. In addition to using references from news headlines and movies to describe operas, all of the opera's promotional materials were redesigned to help create a consistent look—with eye-catching symbols and contemporary colors, such as purple, used on all ads and brochures. Opera attendance jumped by 21% that season. Within four years, Beggs' populist campaign reached a new level, when she introduced coordinated season themes, with each opera tied to a movie title. A new brochure touting "Sneak Previews of the toe-tapping, spine-tingling, heart-wrenching, show-stopping, one-of-a-kind summer festival," described *Carmen* as "fatal attraction," *Susannah* as "the long hot summer," *The Marriage of Figaro* as "risky business" and *La Boheme* as "last tango in Paris," a story in which "four hippies in a Parisian pad make

A billboard promoting the Cincinnati Opera's season, tied in to the film *Pretty Woman*.

love—not war." The movie link proved so appealing to audiences that in following seasons a single movie title was used as each season's theme—*Fatal Attraction, Pretty Woman,* and *Only the Lonely,* among them—with each opera chosen to fit the theme. A *Spellbound* campaign not only tied in to the movie but was linked to Estee Lauder's introduction of a new perfume by that name—with the cosmetics firm providing marketing and promotional support to the opera company.

RESULT: Since adopting the new promotional approach, the opera company has won tremendous national as well as local media attention. Ticket sales have soared as well. Since the campaign began, attendance has averaged over 95%, with subscription renewal rates of over 85%.

6

YOUTH MUST BE SERVED:

Thematic Approach Taps Younger Audience

CHALLENGE: Many arts groups, especially symphony orchestras, concerned with the "graying" of their audiences, have used a range of programmatic and promotional techniques over the years to attract younger people to their presentations. One group, the New York City-based American Symphony Orchestra, was somewhat alarmed to discover that its average audience age was fifty-five. Committed to innovative programming, the orchestra attempted to connect audience interest in other areas with classical music. The result was programs such as "Surrealism and Music? The Musical World Around René Magritte" and, the following season, "The Breakup of the Soviet Union: A Musical Mirror (1980-1990)," with promotional material for the latter program aimed at students from Columbia University's School of International Affairs.

PLAN: When a follow-up survey showed an average subscription-audience age of only forty-five, with 25% under forty, the orchestra knew it was on the right track. Because the same survey showed that many respondents wanted a ticket purchase-plan more flexible than traditional subscriptions, the orchestra sought a new approach while remaining committed to thematic programming.

SUNDAY, SEPTEMBER 25, 1994   3:00 P.M.

PARIS
in the 1860s
The Origins of Impressionism
(in conjunction with the Metropolitan Museum of Art)

Leon Botstein, Conductor

J. Offenbach   La Vie Parisienne (1866)
(Opera-buffa in four Acts - a concert performance)

In conjunction with a major exhibition entitled "The Origins of Impressionism" featuring paintings from the 1860s, which will open at the Metropolitan Museum in the fall, the ASO will present a complete concert performance of Jacques Offenbach's 1866 operetta La Vie Parisienne.

An uproarious satire reflecting new cosmopolitan sensibilities, La Vie Parisienne, which has a libretto by one of the painter Edgar Degas's closest friends, Ludovic Halevy, was Offenbach's greatest commercial success in Europe and America.

One of the thematic concerts offered by the American Symphony Orchestra.

RESULT: In a flier headed "Don't Subscribe to the American Symphony Orchestra," ticket buyers were offered membership in "First Call," a program which allowed them to buy two tickets for the price of one for each concert, once they had paid a $25 fee. Buyers responded to the offer and the season's thematic programming, which included "Bruckner and 20th-Century Politics" and "Paris in the 1860s: The Origins of Impressionism," presented in conjunction with the Metropolitan Museum of Art. Some 400 members signed up for First Call, at what executive director Eugene Carr termed "a cost of less-than 20% of what the orchestra formerly spent to bring in new subscribers."

7

RENEW—ON THIS NIGHT ONLY:

Free Event Helps Sell Entire Season

CHALLENGE: Faced with the opportunity that a major anniversary presents, most arts groups rise to the occasion. The Centre for the Arts at Brock University in St. Catharines, Ontario, Canada was no exception as it celebrated its twenty-fifth anniversary season with critical acclaim and near-record attendance. As it started planning for its twenty-sixth season, however, the staff wondered how it could repeat what it had just accomplished, especially when the artists for the upcoming season, while equally talented and exciting, weren't the recognizable "names" of the prior year.

PLAN: Managing director Debbie Slade and her staff decided that they had to create an aura of excitement and strike quickly with some dramatic offering. The result was a mailing inviting 1,700 subscribers or single-ticket buyers from the previous season to a special free evening at the Centre, just for them. "If you like saving money, free entertainment, classic wines and good food," the letter stated in its opening paragraph, "then you won't want to miss the excitement at the Centre for the Arts." The letter emphasized that, in addition to the entertainment, refreshments, backstage tours and door prizes, "**on this night only** you will receive a **30% discount** off your ticket order if you buy four or more shows." The letter stressed the need to act quickly, since seating was limited, and the 565-seat house was packed to capacity. Arriving guests were treated to artist displays in the lobby and videos and recordings of the coming season's performers before being seated in the auditorium. The program itself included a preview of the coming season and its guest artists, presented by Ms. Slade. The audience was then invited into the lobby, where refreshments were offered and tickets were sold.

RESULT: During a two-hour period, months in advance of the next season's start, the Centre sold 26% of its total ticket inventory, taking in $26,000—25% of its projected box office income. The campaign wasn't over, though. Days after the event, 1,400 follow-up letters were mailed to patrons who did *not* attend, offering them a 25% discount off the purchase of four or more shows if they responded within a month. The mailing brought in an additional twenty-eight ticket orders. Another fifty letters mailed to patrons who attended the free event but did not buy tickets, drew seven more ticket orders, plus an indication by five others that indeed they *had* renewed, but under another person's name. Combined, these two follow-ups generated an additional $16,600 in ticket sales. Overall, in fewer than six weeks, 38% of the season's tickets were sold. "When comparing this season with the anniversary season the year before," said Slade, "in terms of income generated and ticket sales, we were right on the money."

8

THE ART OF SUBSCRIPTION:

Artists Design Brochures

CHALLENGE: The Joyce Theater in New York City, one of America's best-known dance spaces, was looking for a new and exciting concept for its subscription brochure. Because the theatre presented a diverse group of thirty or more dance companies during Fall and Spring seasons every year, it needed an attention-getting piece with quality artwork that could tie together each of the seasons through a unifying theme.

PLAN: The Joyce commissioned a talented artist, David Garner, to create original art based on a theme developed in collaboration with Joyce personnel. Garner created twelve watercolors on the theme "Leap Year," showing dancers in motion. Since then, the Joyce has commissioned a single artist every year to produce original art for its brochures, based on such specific themes as "Windows on Dance" and "Bold Strokes."

RESULT: Audience response was excellent, with many ticket buyers taking the trouble to indicate how much they enjoyed the brochures. While brochures alone can't sell a season, they were one of the factors that helped trigger a jump in paid attendance from 74% to 82% in the first year, and that has helped attendance to remain above 80% since. Artist commissions have increased brochure production costs slightly, but there's been a compensating factor—the establishment of a consistent calendar format. While the artwork often differs dramatically from year to year, the size and look of the brochures are the same, so they are always identifiable as the very distinctive Joyce publication.

Artist Ed Koren's illustration for a Joyce Theater season brochure.

9

A Happy Face:

Cartoons Promote Ticket Sales

CHALLENGE: Arts groups are constantly striving to put on a happy face to appear more approachable and friendly. The Cincinnati Symphony, seeking to broaden its appeal to a wider audience base, had a happy face in its community to turn to for assistance: nationally-known *Cincinnati Enquirer* editorial cartoonist Jim Borgman. When approached by orchestra marketing director Dianne L. Cooper for his help, Borgman agreed to donate his services. Coincidentally, the very next day Borgman won the Pulitzer Prize for his editorial cartoons.

PLAN: The promotion was launched with Borgman's cover design for the season brochure, linking two season highlights—the orchestra's focus on Mozart's music and the 500th anniversary of Columbus's discovery of America. The full-color cover showed "Christopher and Amadeus," who would "take a lot of bows at Music Hall this season." Other Borgman cartoons also appeared in the brochure. To capitalize on Borgman's popularity in the community it was decided—with Borgman's approval—that his role would be a recurring one throughout the season. Thus, a new Borgman cartoon, appearing on Fridays, lightly illustrated each weekend's concert themes.

RESULT: By promoting concerts in a friendly and entertaining manner, Borgman's cartoons proved effective in generating interest in the orchestra. Readers not only looked at the cartoons but actually sought them out. In addition to the many positive comments the orchestra received, there was a pragmatic result: single-ticket sales during the season increased by 15%.

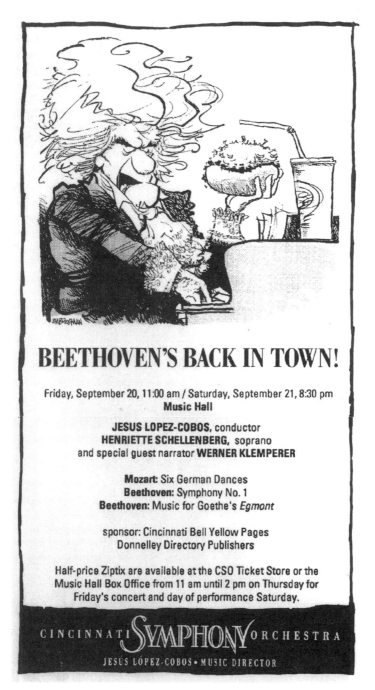

A Cincinnati Symphony ad using an original drawing by prize-winning cartoonist Jim Borgman.

10

Sell...or Else:

Local Reference Attracts Audiences

CHALLENGE: The Winston-Salem Symphony Guild, the volunteer arm of the orchestra, was confronted with a nearly impossible challenge. With the symphony due to move into a new home at the Stevens Center the following year, conductor Peter Perret wanted to make its last season at the 1900-seat Reynolds Auditorium a memorable one. He told the Guild that it had to sell out the house or he would resign.

PLAN: The Symphony Guild took the maestro at his word, or almost at his word. It recognized that while every seat didn't have to be sold, the house, at least, had to be nearly full. Seeking a promotional concept that would sell, the Guild came up with a campaign theme designed to attract the interest and attention of local audiences. Utilizing a familiar Southern image, the ticket-selling campaign designed by a local ad agency was built around music by "the good ol' boys." The "boys"—Brahms, Beethoven and Mozart—were featured in subscription brochures and campaign literature.

RESULT: According to Janet Fox, the current Symphony marketing director, it was indeed a sell-out season. "The Symphony did well enough so that the Maestro Perret didn't leave," she said. In fact, as of this writing, Maestro Perret was still on the Symphony podium.

11

The Politics of Opera:

Elected Official Draws Audience

CHALLENGE: The Connecticut Opera had an avid opera fan in its midst, who attracted attention for reasons other than his love of music. If, surmised the opera company, it could find a logical way to involve Connecticut's Governor Lowell Weicker in its program,

Weicker—with his propensity for the spotlight—would help generate tremendous publicity for the opera's upcoming non-traditional production of *Madama Butterfly*.

PLAN: The opera company suggested that if the Governor would make his operatic debut in its *Butterfly*, it would invent a non-singing role for him as a commanding officer. After agreement by Weicker, the publicity wheels were set in motion for five distinct promotional opportunities: the announcement; a photo call featuring "Madama Butterfly" visiting the Governor in his office; mentions of his debut in Weicker's press conferences; advance event coverage; and coverage of the actual performance.

RESULT: The Governor's appearance generated more press than any event in the company's forty-nine-year history, not only at the state and local level but nationally and internationally. Stories and photos appeared on both the Associated Press and UPI wires and in such national periodicals as *Newsweek*, helping boost single-ticket sales by 313% over the company's most recent previous production of *Butterfly*. The opera company also won a new supporter—the Governor. In fact, eight months later Governor Weicker—by now a veteran performer—agreed to appear in another Connecticut Opera production, its irreverent slapstick production of *The Barber of Seville*, updated to the 1920s. Since the Governor had recently pushed through an unpopular state income tax, the opera company incorporated—with the Governor's approval—an extra bit of tomfoolery to allow taxpayers to get their revenge: he'd get hit with a pie in the face during the performance by two voters selected through a well-publicized contest. The publicity was even greater this second time around, including notice in the *New York Times*, the *Wall Street Journal*, *Time* magazine, *USA Today* and on the wire services. While the opera company reaped tremendous attention and helped dispel the stereotype of opera as boring, it also didn't hurt itself at the box office. Single-ticket sales were 25% above projections.

$$\overline{12}$$

WITH A LITTLE BIT OF HELP:

Maximizing Small Grant

CHALLENGE: The Signature Theatre Company, a small Off-Off-Broadway troupe, was in desperate need of its first subscription brochure. When a talented designer offered to contribute her services to create the brochure, all that was needed was money to pay printing costs. The company, whose annual budget was only $90,000, explored all possible funding avenues and drew up a list of options in case grants it had applied for didn't come through.

PLAN: When the company won a $1,000 grant from the first cycle of the new Nancy Quinn Emerging Theatre Fund Awards, it was ready to move ahead. Although the total funding was small, it covered the entire cost of printing 8,000 black-and-white brochures. With the remaining funds and some money of its own, the company mailed brochures to the 5,000 names it had accumulated over prior seasons, offering recipients the opportunity to purchase performance passes, good for four plays, for the price of three, beginning at $45 a pass. To raise additional funds the company offered passes at four higher levels—$75, $125, $200, and $300—with benefits added at each level for contributions above the $45 base price.

RESULT: The first-time mailing resulted in a 384% increase in passes sold, from 40 to 192. Advance ticket income was $8,600 and an additional $1,000 was raised from pass buyers in higher categories. Buoyed by its success, Signature undertook a second mailing the next season with even better results: sales tripled. The budget had risen to $210,000 and income from 607 passes sold rose to $29,000 and passholder donations increased to $5,495.

Signature Theatre Company

invites you to join us for our 4th exciting season. The only theatre in the country that dedicates each season to the exploration of a single playwright's body of work, Signature is pleased to announce The 1994-95 Horton Foote Season. Mr. Foote's distinguished career spans regional theatre, Off-Broadway, Broadway, television and film. He is possibly best known as the writer of the Academy Award-winning films *To Kill A Mockingbird* with Gregory Peck, *Tender Mercies* with Robert Duvall, and *A Trip To Bountiful* with Geraldine Page. The world of Horton Foote shimmers with the exquisite richness and drama of the explosions just beneath the surface of quiet lives. Come celebrate with us the beauty that Mr. Foote finds in the details of life, and the triumphs of his unforgettable characters.

"That is the kind of discovery the Signature Theatre permits by consecrating each season to one playwright alone. Instead of looking at plays as piecemeal goods we're encouraged to view them as part of a larger body of work, as extensions and reflections of one another. It is a far more fruitful approach to theater than the hit-or-miss ethic that prevails elsewhere."

- David Richards,
The New York Times

L-R: Austin Pendleton in Romulus Linney's *The Sorrows Of Frederick*; Tom Klunis and Kathleen Butler in Edward Albee's *The Marriage Play*; Keith Reddin and Samantha Mathis in Lee Blessing's *Fortinbras*
All photos: Susan Johann

Signature Theatre Company • **James Houghton,** Founding Artistic Director • **Thomas C. Proehl,** Managing Director
Performing at Kampo Cultural and Multi-Media Center • **31 Bond Street, New York, NY** • **(212) 967-1913**

A Signature Theatre Company brochure.

Chapter Five

Outrageous Promotions

1

RECOGNIZING A PROMOTIONAL OPPORTUNITY:

Spoof Promotes Art

CHALLENGE: The Detroit Institute of Arts was about to reopen its newly renovated nineteenth-century European Galleries. Since the Galleries had never had their own space before, and since the space included some of the museum's most recognized and best-loved works—including outstanding Impressionist paintings—the museum saw a unique opportunity to promote the reopened galleries as one of the museum's leading attractions. This strategy was somewhat unorthodox, since many museums direct their top promotional efforts to temporary exhibits and events rather than permanent collections.

PLAN: The museum's marketing and public relations staff decided to spoof a popular-music concept and have some fun by promoting the reopening as "Hit Versions by the Original Artists." The playful concept of focusing on "oldies" in the brochure—the reverse side heralded the opening as the date when "The Greatest Hits of the 19th Century are Back"—broadened the appeal of the galleries and museum to a wider audience. According to Cyndi A. Summers, the museum's associate director of marketing and public relations who supervised and coordinated implementation of the campaign, "it also dispelled the image of the DIA as a stuffy or inaccessible place." In addition to the brochure, promotional materials included souvenir buttons, ads, posters, print and broadcast advertising and a media preview.

RESULT: Museum attendance for the three months following the campaign's launching jumped 22%, with a very favorable public response to the creativity of the approach and its departure from the norm. Press coverage of the renovation was extensive and business and marketing media paid special attention to the campaign's focus. The campaign received additional recognition in a competition organized by the Detroit chapter of the International Association of Business Communication when it won an award of Excellence, the top honor in the category of "Most Innovative Communication."

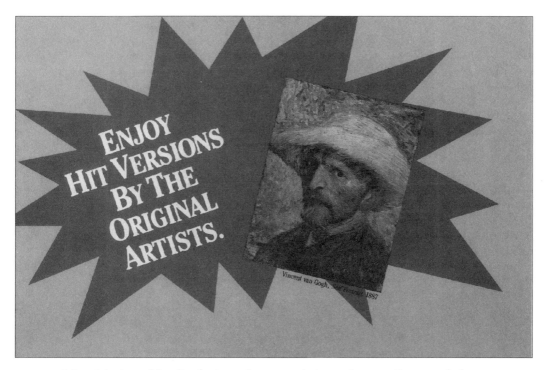

A Detroit Institute of Arts flier for its newly renovated nineteenth-century European Galleries.

2

United We Fund:

Arts Groups Cooperate

CHALLENGE: Recognizing that many arts funders in his city shared common interests, James McClelland, director of development at the Curtis Institute of Music in Philadelphia, thought it would be a good idea if they came together to discuss mutual concerns. Some fifteen of Philadelphia's development directors, representing a broad cross-section of the city's arts groups, began meeting informally for breakfast every month. After months of discussion, and feedback from corporate funders and key local officials invited to meet with the "Development Roundtable" as the group came to be known, it became evident that there was a major problem—the arts in Philadelphia had a poor image and were of minor importance to major funders more concerned with other causes.

PLAN: Roundtable members decided that a program to counter the apathy towards the arts was needed. The dramatic device used to launch the counterattack was a series of four anonymous postcards mailed intermittently over a six-month period to some 5,000 corporate leaders and civic officials. Data used on the cards was researched by Roundtable members with funding provided by three corporate contribution officers who had previously addressed the group and other local businesses. Each of the numbered cards, designed to highlight the significance and impact of local arts programs in a different discipline, asked a question beginning with the phrase, "What U.S. City..." followed by a series of three questions. Card one, for example, asked "What U.S. City: had more theatrical premieres last year than any city outside of New York? Has a $30-million theatre industry, generating $75 million for its local economy? Has more than 2,000 performance nights of professional theatre a year for an audience approaching a million people?" When turned upside down, the card read, "Philadelphia! A Real Theatre Town." Card information also was used by local arts groups, which included the statistics in their printed programs, and by businesses using them as "statement stuffers." First Fidelity Bank's stuffer, for example, reached 450,000 customers. Buoyed by the positive response to the postcard mailings, the Roundtable launched other projects, including cooperative ventures with the local Convention Bureau: a weekend for out-of-town music writers who attended not only major performances but a half-day sampler showcasing many smaller musical groups; and a breakfast meeting with the heads of local arts groups for twenty travel editors.

RESULT: Arts visibility in the city was definitely raised, and telephone inquiries to arts groups increased dramatically, with many converted to ticket sales. Also, according to McClelland, "All this activity and visibility helped pave the way for the City's spectacular Avenue of the Arts project." There were other key results as well; for example, the Dolfinger-McMahon Foundation was so excited by the Roundtable program that it awarded a grant to produce 150,000 copies of a first-time-ever color brochure on local musical groups. Importantly, the dialogue started by the Roundtable has brought many local arts groups together into a working relationship that has spawned new cooperative activity, including a funded pilot for a weekly TV-show on the arts in Philadelphia.

3

NETWORKING—ON TELEVISION:

Winning National Exposure

CHALLENGE: The Portland Opera in Oregon, seeking to break down what it termed "the stereotypic misconception that opera is stuffy," came up with sweatshirts emblazoned with a decidedly unstuffy message—that opera offers "civilized evenings of lust, greed, murder" and much more. Told that Willard Scott of NBC's network TV-show *Today* mentioned on-air that he enjoyed opera, public relations director Jim Fullan decided to see if he could take the opera company campaign for recognition a step further and induce Scott to talk about the Portland Opera on national television.

PLAN: Striking immediately, Fullan called NBC in New York to find out how to reach Scott. Told by a *Today* staff member that anything sent to Scott would be waiting for him on top of his pile when he returned from Washington the next morning, he faxed Scott in Washington to tell him that a rather interesting package would await his arrival in New York. Knowing that Scott enjoyed using props and reasoning that the sweatshirt would demonstrate a quirky humor not usually associated with opera, Fullan sent Scott a sweatshirt along with a letter, commending him on his enjoyment of opera and hoping "you might find a bit of time in one of your weather reports" to mention the opening of the Portland Opera season that week. He also referred to the sweatshirt and its legend—reading "Come enjoy civilized evenings of lust, greed, murder, love triangles and double-crossing. Portland Opera, Anything But Stuffy"— and suggested "Should you be tempted to wear the shirt with that message, all the better for us...and all the better for all the new opera fans you might create."

RESULT: Two mornings later, Scott appeared on the *Today* show wearing the sweatshirt and announcing the opening of the opera season in Portland. Immediately, lightning struck. The opera company received calls from all over the country, both from people wanting to order sweatshirts and from colleagues and opera buffs offering congratulations on the coup. Locally, the effect was tremendous. According to Fullan, "In the eyes of the general public here, we were suddenly 'something,' held a bit higher than they previously considered us, burnished with bronze rather than tarnished with stuffiness. For our subscribers it was a powerful confirmation of their feelings. For our board it was an interesting boost, an energizing shot that gave them something additional to use in furthering our cause." Fullan's advice to arts administrators suddenly confronted with a public relations opportunity is fourfold: "Approach the unknown with questions; frame the pitch in the context of its target; be prepared to act quickly; and deliver what you promised exactly when you promise it."

4

CALL ME A CAB:

Taxicab Drivers Promote Art

CHALLENGE: With the blockbuster exhibition, "Claude Monet: Impressionist Masterpieces from the Museum of Fine Arts, Boston," set to open later in the week, the Baltimore Museum of Art wanted to be sure that everyone knew about the show and where it was being held. Among the potential promoters identified by museum staff members were cab drivers who, having seen the exhibition, could then recommend it to their fares.

PLAN: Five days before the exhibition opened to the public, the museum held Cab Driver Appreciation Day, with drivers invited to stop by the museum for a free bag lunch, a Monet/BMA button and the opportunity to preview the exhibition. Fliers announcing the invitation were sent to all of Baltimore's cab companies.

Cab Driver Appreciation Day at the Baltimore Museum of Art.

RESULT: The event drew a good turnout and an enthusiastic response from the cabbies. Indicative of the promotion's success was the story related to the museum staff by the director of The Museum of Fine Arts, Boston, who came to Baltimore for the exhibition opening. When he told a cab driver to take him to the museum, the driver responded, "Oh, you must be going to see Monet at the BMA. You're going to love those paintings." The promotion has a secondary benefit as well: In addition to the cab drivers, newspaper reporters and television-camera crews turned out for the event creating a flurry of advance publicity. Riding on a strong promotional wave, the exhibition—over its run of nearly three months—drew 215,000 viewers, nearly doubling the museum's attendance record for a single exhibition.

5

ON BASE:

Promotional Tie-in to Play's Theme

CHALLENGE: Baseball isn't the everyday subject of theatre; but, considering the media coverage it receives, it's worth an extra promotional effort when a script is built around the sport. Such an opportunity presented itself to San Diego's Old Globe Theatre when it produced *Mr. Rickey Calls a Meeting*, a play based on Jackie Robinson's breakthrough as the first black person to play major-league baseball.

PLAN: Looking for a special promotional angle, the theatre contacted a local sports organization, the San Diego Sports Hall of Champions, and was able to arrange for them to mount a special exhibit about the Negro Leagues—the league in which Jackie Robinson began his career—to coincide with the Old Globe production. The Hall also agreed to do a group promotion to its members, offering $5 discounts for tickets on specific "working person's weekday matinees." The theatre also developed special promotions with the city's major-league baseball team, the San Diego Padres, including $5 off theatre tickets with stubs from Padres' games promoted on the stadium scoreboard, and arranged for the NAACP to sell tickets to two performances designated as fund-raisers. A real promotional breakthrough came when an article about former players in the Negro Leagues appeared in the *Los Angeles Times*. The theatre staff was quick to react, tracking down two of the former players mentioned— Merle Porter and Sammie Haynes—of the Kansas City Monarchs, Jackie Robinson's old team. Through Porter and Haynes and a former San Diego sportswriter, the theatre reached other former Negro Leagues players and invited them, along with Porter and Haynes, to a special tour of the Hall of Champions exhibit and a luncheon following it. Since the theatre had done a play with a baseball theme several years earlier, it was able to update its list of sports writers and invite them to meet and interview the former players at the exhibit and luncheon. Following the luncheon, the players and sportswriters attended *Mr. Rickey Calls a Meeting* at the Old Globe and a reception for the players that followed.

RESULT: The Old Globe promotion received tremendous attention in the sports pages of local newspaper and on local television, with Porter and Haynes proving to be remarkable interviewees. Virtually all the sports stories included major references to the Old Globe production. Carried on a wave of publicity, *Mr. Rickey* sold 92% of the house with complete sell-outs in its final weeks. Apparently, the theatre's love affair with baseball continued. Several years later, its production of *Damn Yankees*, following a successful run in San Diego, reopened in Broadway and became a hit.

6

MARKETING AN OPPORTUNITY:

Using National Spotlight Locally

CHALLENGE: The Concerto Soloists Chamber Orchestra of Philadelphia was presented with a unique opportunity when it was invited to perform at one of the four inaugural dinners for President Bill Clinton in Washington, DC. Although the orchestra would be reaping national exposure, it wanted to utilize the honor to go one step further and win extra promotional attention in its home city, Philadelphia. The best spot for local attention-getting—and certainly the most visible—was the top of the Philadelphia Electric Company building, the giant lights of which flash electric messages that are seen throughout the city.

PLAN: Because of its visibility, there is great competition to be featured atop the Electric Company building. The orchestra had an "in" with the company, however, and decided that this was the time to use it. One of the volunteers working on an orchestra gala was a former employee of the Electric Company, and he used his connection to win approval on short notice for the orchestra to be featured in lights.

RESULT: While the orchestra was performing in the main hall of the National Building Museum for 1,400 guests, its special honor was being recognized in Philadelphia—in very bright lights.

7

LOCAL IDENTITY:

Identifying with Home Community

CHALLENGE: The Miami String Quartet, first-prize winner of the Concert Artists Guild 1992 Competition, was seeking a way to identify with Miami, where they had been in residency with the New World School of the Arts for several years. The challenge to the Concert Artists Guild, which books their tours, was to identify them as serious musicians while dramatizing their youth, sense of fun and willingness to take chances.

PLAN: A new photo of the quartet, showing them in evening dress on a Miami beach, became their official publicity picture, featured in brochures and sent to presenters for use in cities where they were appearing. In addition to the casual irreverence of the beach photo, the group broke with tradition

The Miami String Quartet's official publicity photo.

by being photographed *without* their musical instruments, indicating to audiences and presenters that they were willing to try new things.

RESULT: The press response was immediate and generous, with virtually every newspaper in cities where the quartet performed using the photo. Also, according to Katie Knowles, Concert Artist Guild press representative, "Concert presenters love this photo. It's usually featured in every season brochure when the quartet participates in a series. In Minnesota, one presenter promoted their recital in February as 'Miami Comes to Minnesota,' which caught the attention of everyone in the sub-zero weather. The photo has been good for the group and presenters and it definitely has made it easier to promote the group to potential presenters because it almost guarantees press coverage."

8

Standing on Ceremony: The Marriage Kind:

Radio Station Tie-in

CHALLENGE: Because *The Marriage of Figaro* is a familiar, frequently-produced opera, it's often difficult for a regional opera company to find new ways to promote it. Looking for an unusual marketing concept to help sell its production, the Connecticut Opera seized on one interesting aspect of *Figaro*: In spite of its title, no wedding ceremony takes place in the opera.

PLAN: Without changing the opera in any way, the company decided to add a real wedding to *The Marriage of Figaro*, immediately in advance of the performance. Looking to attract younger audiences, the opera troupe proposed a tie-in to a local Top 40 radio station noted for its outrageous promotions. The station, KISS 95.7, heavily promoted a contest to find a couple who would be wed onstage an hour before curtain time on opening night—before an audience of operagoers. In return for the free wedding and a honeymoon donated by various merchants, the winning couple would agree to extensive interviews and photo sessions.

RESULT: In addition to a no-cost promotional barrage on KISS (the station received its highest ratings ever during the promotion), the wedding received wide local print and television coverage as well as national attention from wire services and a feature story as "The Wedding of the Year" on the nationally syndicated TV-show, *A Current Affair*. Single-ticket sales doubled advance projections, with many younger adults—the KISS audience—among the ticket buyers.

9

ANYTHING BUT DULL:

Fun Way to Get Noticed

CHALLENGE: Since many people perceive the arts as stuffy, the Mississippi Arts Commission, an official state arts agency, was looking for a new and entertaining way to tell state residents about the Commission and its activities and to cast what it termed "a friendly light on the arts world." Jane Hiatt, the Commission's director, reasoned that "If we had a little fun with a brochure, people who normally might not read this kind of material just might look at it."

PLAN: The agency contracted with one of the state's top graphic designers to come up with a new brochure that would be lively, fun and readable. Eight months in planning, the twelve-page, 11" by 17" brochure featured a stern-looking police trooper on its address side—with a legend next to him reading "Warning! Your life is about to get more exciting!"—and offbeat photos—a cow and the Statue of Liberty among them—and upbeat tongue-in-cheek copy inside. In the same light spirit, the brochure included two pages promoting the offer of a free copy of another Arts Commission publication, its guide to programs and services entitled, "Dull Reading That Can Make Your Life More Exciting."

RESULT: The $6,825 spent on printing 2,000 brochures was well worth the cost. Designed for use over a two-year period as mailing pieces and for distribution at arts events, the brochure has given the agency a lot of attention and has resulted in unsolicited letters and calls commending the agency's effort.

We can help you financially.

The Mississippi Arts Commission funds activities that promote public understanding and support of arts and culture. We give grants to artists or organizations for workshops and residencies, coordination of arts events, performances, services to artists and arts organizations, artistic and managerial development and arts in education programs.

We want to recognize artistic excellence in your area.

The Governor's Awards for Excellence in the Arts officially recognizes those whose work in the arts has contributed significantly to the development of Mississippi cultural life. Each year outstanding artists, patrons, arts organizations and businesses are recognized at a televised ceremony which celebrates the arts and artists in Mississippi.

We can teach you how to make life more exciting.

The Commission offers a statewide conference on the arts or regional conferences in alternate years to address issues affecting the arts. Presenting artists, arts in education, board development, planning, cultural diversity, and grant writing are just a few of the topics. Watch your mailbox for more information on upcoming conferences.

Call for our grant deadlines. There's a program to benefit every community.

Jane Crater Hiatt
Executive Director

Here's our phone number one more time. Big. Because we want you to call. 601-359-6030.

Edwin E. Downer
Chair

Mississippi Arts Commission's "fun" brochure.

10

Dog Day Afternoon:

Live Animals Win Press Attention

CHALLENGE: During a season when subscription sales were flat, the Lyric Opera of Kansas City sought ways to boost ticket sales through news-making promotions.

PLAN: The opera company decided to capitalize on its upcoming production of Friedrich von Flotow's *Martha*; set in England, the opera includes a hunt scene that gave the promotional staff an idea. Why not, they thought, stage a "Beagle Audition" ten days before opening, at a downtown park only a block from the theater? When the director agreed to use several dogs in the production, the stage was set. A press release mailed two weeks prior to the event, headlined "The Opera Needs a Few Good Beagles," attracted considerable attention from the local press. The event itself, drew coverage from every local television station, four newspapers and three radio stations as well as national and international notice from the BBC, which did a phone interview with the director, and the *Today* show, which included mention in its newscast. At the audition, which drew thirty-seven beagles, each dog received a numbered card, dog food, and a doggie bag while their owners received free Lyric Opera key chains. Auditions included walking in groups and alone, meeting "Martha" and listening to music from the opera. Nine winning dogs, who received standard AGMA contracts for dogs, paying $3 a performance to cover parking, "signed" with their paw prints.

RESULT: Riding on a wave of publicity, the opera sold 2,000 single tickets, topping all but one other opera that season in the number of group and single tickets sold.

11

THE ISSUE IS CENSORSHIP:

Promoting a Controversial Topic

CHALLENGE: Monroe Community College in Rochester, New York launched an ambitious year-long educational program on censorship with a good part of the focus on the arts. Because the program (which included a film series, poster exhibition, readings and symposia) was designed to reach as large an audience as possible, its planners needed effective ways to promote the concept.

PLAN: A pack of fifteen "censorship trading cards" was introduced, with attendees given cards at each of the programs they attended. Among the censored figures in literature and the arts featured on the cards were such notables of the past as D.H. Lawrence, James Joyce and Oscar Wilde; contemporary figures included Karen Finley, Lenny Bruce and Madonna. Attendees were invited to try to complete a pack by attending additional programs and exchanging duplicates with other attendees.

RESULT: The cards, designed and donated by David Cowles and other artists, achieved their objective by focusing local as well as national attention on the censorship program. *Playboy* was among the publications which picked up the story. The program's poster show traveled to six other venues in New York State, where it triggered discussion and, in some instances, considerable controversy. "The censorship program proved a unifying force for the arts community," said Kathleen Farrell, director of Monroe's Mercer Gallery, who coordinated the trading card project. "We received calls and cards from all over the world."

Censorship trading cards used by Monroe Community College to promote its education program on censorship.

12

Shopping for Audiences:

Arts Promotion at the Supermarket

CHALLENGE: The Evansville Philharmonic Orchestra was looking for ways to promote its season along with its added attraction, a new Family Concert Series sponsored by the City of Evansville. The Orchestra had an extra promotional feature that was worth exploiting: the appearance of the well-known comic-strip character, Garfield the Cat, in the inaugural family concert.

PLAN: The Orchestra arranged for a local supermarket, Schnucks East, to sponsor an in-store Season Kick-Off for the Orchestra. In a Schnucks' ad promoting the event, "Garfield" invited the public to attend. Sackers at Schnucks markets also stuffed invitations into shopping bags. The kick-off featured information tables with sign-ups to win free season tickets; video showings; Garfield displays; and live performances by a woodwind trio near the store entrance, a pianist in the produce areas and a brass trio in the pharmacy. Several months later, Schnucks North brought "Garfield Live" to a celebration promoting the opening Family concert. Shoppers were treated to a visit with Garfield, free hot dogs and root beer floats and, for the kids, face painting and gift balloons. While Garfield was greeting shoppers and issuing invitations to his concert, Evansville Philharmonic musicians performed a selection of ragtime tunes.

RESULT: Both supermarket appearances received tremendous local attention, helping both the regular subscription and Family Series get off to flying starts.

Chapter Six

Advertising Your Worth

1

SCORING A GOAL:

Tongue-in-cheek Ads

CHALLENGE: The Vancouver Opera wanted to counteract a series of ads in periodicals, bus shelters and posters, used by the city's National Hockey League team, the Canucks, to promote the opening of the hockey season. Print ads showing a hockey mask vaguely resembling a *Phantom of the Opera* mask were headlined, "The Opera It's Not." Radio ads promoting the excitement of attending a hockey game ended with the line, "It's not the opera."

PLAN: Recognizing the opportunity to reach new audiences and promote their own season, but having limited resources, the opera company decided to take a lighthearted approach and score some goals in familiar hockey territory. The upshot was a series of four tongue-in-cheek ads, one for each opera in the company's upcoming season, with each of the ads running once in the sports section of the *Vancouver Sun*, a newspaper in which the opera had available sponsorship space. Each ad featured a provocative headline ("The Gloves Are Off!" was the one-liner for *La Traviata*) followed by the promotional line, "Hockey? Surprise—It's opera!" Performance dates and ticket information followed.

RESULT: The opera ad-campaign opened the publicity floodgates with tremendous press coverage given to the tongue-in-cheek "war." It also drew a positive reaction from the publicity-minded Canucks who not only invited opera bass David Pittsinger to face-off against Canuck captain Trever Linden at a scheduled practice with the press on hand—but asked opera company performers to sing the national anthem before a Canucks' nationally televised hockey game.

One of the ads from the Vancouver Opera's tongue-in-cheek campaign.

2

FLY ME TO THE MUSEUM:

In-flight Advertising

CHALLENGE: The Metropolitan Museum of Art was seeking a new way to motivate airline travelers to see its collections when they visited New York City. Since in-flight magazines and audiotapes were read and heard by millions of passengers, museum officials thought that a combination of the two could provide them with an effective promotional and educational vehicle.

PLAN: Museum officials approached Pan American Airlines with an unusual idea: that it publish an insert on the Metropolitan's permanent collection in its *Clipper* magazine and combine it with a corresponding audiotape that would run continuously on one of the airline's audio channels. Pan Am liked the idea, and since it changed its audio selections every three months, it agreed to use a tape on the museum throughout one summer season. A thirty-minute audio tour of sixteen major works in the museum's collection, narrated by museum director Philippe de Montebello, was paired with a six-page feature in the *Clipper*, prepared by the museum design department and submitted as advertising pages, showing full-color photos of the works described by Mr. de Montebello in his narrative.

RESULT: With an estimated *Clipper* readership of 1.3 million a month, the promotion attracted widespread attention and helped boost traveler awareness of the breadth and quality of the museum's permanent collection. Pan Am, which unfortunately has since ceased operations, told the museum that the program was one of the most innovative ideas it had seen in the travel field in recent years.

3

ANNIVERSARY SONG:

Bogus Newspaper Attracts Space Buyers

CHALLENGE: The Brooklyn Academy of Music (BAM) was poised to launch the public phase of the first endowment campaign in its 132-year history, a drive to raise $22.5 million in four years. It needed a dramatic way to focus on the major achievements during its "current era"—the twenty-five years since president and executive producer, Harvey Lichtenstein, took over leadership of the institution—and to announce the start of "The Campaign for BAM."

PLAN: BAM decided to tie in the official announcement to a gala free event underwritten by former BAM board presidents, celebrating Lichtenstein's twenty-five years at the helm, with additional funds to be raised through the sale of advertising space in a special tabloid to be published by *New York Newsday*. Months in advance, BAM prepared a tongue-in-cheek cover sheet, with rates and specs on the reverse side, designed to lure major advertisers to the tabloid chronicling "The Harvey Years." Headlines for the dummy cover included "Elvis Responds to BAM's Call For Testimonials" and "Alien Spaceship Lands on Opera House Stage."

A page from the Brooklyn Academy of Music newspaper chronicling "The Harvey Years."

RESULT: The event attracted a full house of BAM supporters and provided a launching pad to announce the endowment campaign and initial gifts and pledges totaling $10.3 million. The forty-eight-page tabloid distributed at the party also made a big hit with the audience. *BAMStar*, in addition to testimonials from elected officials, colleagues and supporters, included "Harvey" comics, a gossip page and songs and poems in tribute to Lichtenstein. Importantly, $90,000 was raised from the sale of tabloid ads.

4

AD AGENCY HELPS BOOST MEMBERSHIP:

Pro Bono Advertising

CHALLENGE: The Asheville, North Carolina Art Museum, with a limited budget, wanted to boost its membership through a new campaign. It was particularly interested in breaking down barriers and reaching audiences who were unfamiliar with it and its collection.

PLAN: The museum turned to a local ad agency, Price-McNabb, for help. The agency, recognizing the opportunity to create the kind of all-out campaign that would showcase its creativity, agreed to provide its services on a pro-bono basis. The agency decided on a lighthearted approach, including the use of popular figures and images familiar to the audience it was trying to reach. Although the campaign included print and TV ads, direct mail and billboards, the only cost to the museum was the installation of the billboards, since the media—including the *Asheville Citizen Times*—donated ad space.

The Asheville Art Museum used this ad to help boost membership.

RESULT: The campaign, which ran most of a year, was a tremendous success, resulting in a 36% increase in new museum memberships. The fun aspects of the ads—including one that said "Don't let your kids grow up thinking Art is just Paul Simon's ex-partner," and a billboard that proclaimed, "Put yourself in our permanent collection," created considerable local comment as well. Every piece used in the campaign ended with the campaign theme, "Join the Asheville Art Museum." Importantly, the advertising agency was just as pleased as the museum with the campaign's success. In addition to local recognition, it won several advertising awards for the effort.

5

HOMETOWN PRIDE:

Stretching Ad Budget

CHALLENGE: The J.B. Speed Art Museum in Louisville, KY was looking for ways to substantially boost attendance. With a $100,000 budget for advertising and promotion approved by its board, the museum invited thirty-four ad agencies to submit presentations. In its winning presentation, Fessel, Siegfreidt & Moeller stressed that it could triple the value of any purchased television time or space because it already had won commitments from local television stations to donate an additional spot for every one purchased and an additional two free billboards for every three purchased.

PLAN: The winning agency, which had provided pro-bono services to the museum in past years, pulled out all the stops to develop a campaign designed to instill local pride in the museum and win new audiences. Based on the theme, "This is Your Art Collection," the campaign included a series of television spots and billboards that were eye-catching and lighthearted. For the spots, the ad agency selected forty-five volunteers, out of 250 who responded, to appear in three thirty-second commercials designed to dramatize the museum's importance to the people of the city. The voice-over to a spot featuring Mayor Jerry Abramson, for example, stated "If you live in the Louisville area, you own one of the finest art collections in America. Visit your art collection soon at the J.B. Speed Art Museum." Billboards, showing works in the museum's collection, featured such tag lines as "Rally 'round your Rubens," "Peek in on your Picasso," and "Rendezvous with your Rembrandt." To demonstrate its concern for the community, the museum kicked off a new admission policy at the campaign's start, waiving all admission charges for its permanent collection.

RESULT: The high-intensity campaign made a tremendous impact on the community. During the six months it ran, museum attendance increased by 64% over a similar period during the previous year. Also, with the agency donating most of its services and other companies providing free or low-cost TV equipment rental, out-of-pocket expenses were less than $1,000.

Ads featured in the J.B. Speed Art Museum's campaign.

$\overline{\underline{6}}$

INSTRUMENTAL TO SUCCESS:

Teaser Ads Boost Awareness

CHALLENGE: The New York Philharmonic was approaching a milestone, its 150th anniversary season. While there was major fanfare surrounding the event, the staff recognized that there was nothing automatic about subscription sales. In fact, as it assessed its marketing strategy, it realized that while the then-current season had an excellent subscriber renewal rate, the acquisition drive for new subscribers was disappointing, perhaps due in part to the fact that potential audiences were unfamiliar with the newly-appointed music director, Kurt Masur. Recognizing a need, the marketing department set as its goal an acquisition campaign as effective as the renewal campaign.

PLAN: Since past experience showed that a major advertisement targeted to new subscribers needed multiple exposures to bring results, the Philharmonic devised a series of four small teaser ads, lighthearted in tone and each featuring a musical instrument. The teasers—mentioning the anniversary season and including an 800 phone number for season brochure requests—ran in the *New York Times* on each of the four Sundays prior to the appearance of a major ad on the fifth Sunday: a two-page spread with full subscription information and order forms.

RESULT: Leads generated were up from the previous year, although precise figures are unavailable. The two-page acquisition ad, following the teasers, did exceptionally well. The Philharmonic more than met its goal, with 1,130 new seats sold, up from 202 the previous year.

One of the ads used by the New York Philharmonic to "drum up" subscriber excitement.

7

BANKING ON TIME:

Arts Support Raises Local Business Profile

CHALLENGE: New Zealand's Hawke's Bay Cultural Trust constantly was on the alert for ways to promote the major museums it administered in two adjacent cities—one in Napier and the other in Hastings. When the Trust's executive director, Roger Smith, learned that the Auckland-based ASB Bank was to begin a nationwide regional expansion and that Napier and Hastings would be among the new sites, he saw a tremendous opportunity for the Trust.

PLAN: Anticipating the bank's need to establish a community profile, Smith immediately approached ASB's regional manager. In return for the bank's annual contribution of $7,800 (NZ)—to cover the cost of producing and inserting illustrated advertisements in evening newspapers for each new exhibition at the Napier and Hastings museums— the Trust would offer specific benefits to the bank: a plaque acknowledging the contribution in the lobby of the Hawke's Bay Museum, Napier; a corporate evening free-of-charge at either museum; and a complimentary ad in the museum-quarterly Friends newsletter, mailed to 1,700 subscribers, with a tag line reading "ASB Bank, proud to support the arts in Hawke's Bay."

RESULT: By acting quickly, the Hawke's Bay Cultural Trust was able to establish a positive ongoing relationship with ASB. Pleased with its partnership with the museums and their audiences, the bank held its corporate evening in conjunction with a major Trust event—the annual review of local art. With its invited guests, the bank brought an extra audience into the Hawke's Bay Museum, Napier, on opening night, swelling event attendance to more than 400 and boosting word-of-mouth publicity. The bank reviewed its sponsorship the following year, deciding to host the review opening—this time in Hastings, at the Hawke's Bay Exhibition Centre—for 350 attendees. As a result of the relationship, the bank and the Trust established a dialogue which has led to discussion of bank sponsorship of other major museum projects.

North Carolina Shakespeare Festival's attention-getting poster.

8

JUST ONE OF THE BOYS:

Selling Shakespeare

CHALLENGE: For his first season as artistic director of the North Carolina Shakespeare Festival, Louis Rackoff wanted to create productions that were accessible to audiences and would relate Shakespeare to North Carolina and the local environment.

PLAN: Since advertising executive Lee Trone was on the Festival's board and his agency, Trone Advertising, was handling most of the theatre's marketing on a pro-bono basis, Rackoff turned to the firm for its help in conveying the message of accessibility. Trone developed a poster that conveyed the concept through the image: Shakespeare attired in unmistakable North Carolina garb—a flannel shirt and a feed cap emblazoned with the Festival logo.

RESULT: The overall result was very positive, with the poster generating what the festival termed "a significant amount of public attention." While the theatre group viewed the poster as a good way to relate Shakespeare to the local lifestyle, there was, nonetheless, an unanticipated minority reaction: Some people thought that NCSF was making fun of the "common" rural image.

1

ENTICING THE NEW DONOR:

Low-Budget Campaign for Small Donors

CHALLENGE: The Tiny Mythic Theater Company in New York City was looking for an offbeat and inexpensive way to attract new low-level donors, people who had had prior involvement with the theatre but had never made a contribution. By asking them for small gifts at first, the theatre reasoned, they could be encouraged to increase their donations over time.

PLAN: With the help of its advertising agency, Mad Dogs and Englishmen, the theatre launched a four-postcard direct-mail campaign to its entire mailing list of 3,000 names. A new card was mailed every month or two; but once someone made a contribution, they stopped receiving cards. Humor was a key ingredient, with one of the cards showing favorable quotes about the theatre followed by a line reading, "Where's my goddam rent?" signed by "Phil the Landlord." On the address side were five lines for contributions, ranging from" $5 (I'm not feeling particularly generous)" to $10, $20 and $25, followed by "More (I can write this off, right?)" At the bottom of the card, the theatre noted that donors of more than $100 would receive gifts. The final line read, "If you give more than $500, we'll marry you and bear your children."

RESULT: According to co-artistic director Tim Maner, the campaign, which cost about $800, was a tremendous success, with more than 100 new donors attracted to the theatre. In spite of its unusual offer to larger donors, however, the theatre reported that no new offspring had been born.

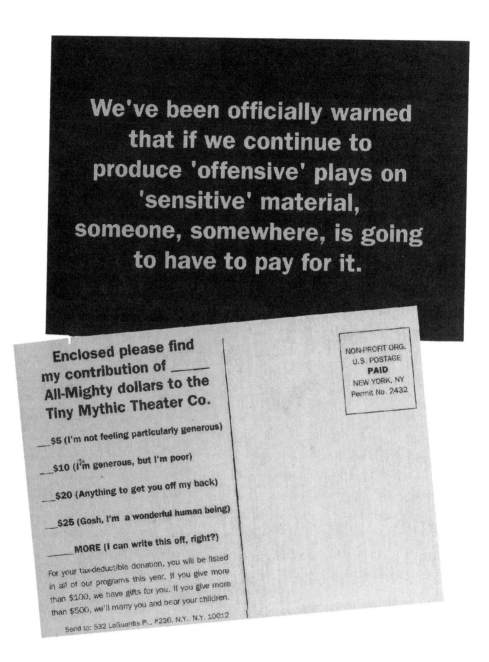

We've been officially warned that if we continue to produce 'offensive' plays on 'sensitive' material, someone, somewhere, is going to have to pay for it.

Enclosed please find my contribution of _____ All-Mighty dollars to the Tiny Mythic Theater Co.

___ $5 (I'm not feeling particularly generous)

___ $10 (I'm generous, but I'm poor)

___ $20 (Anything to get you off my back)

___ $25 (Gosh, I'm a wonderful human being)

_____ MORE (I can write this off, right?)

For your tax-deductible donation, you will be listed in all of our programs this year. If you give more than $100, we have gifts for you. If you give more than $500, we'll marry you and bear your children.

Send to: 532 LaGuardia Pl., #226, N.Y., N.Y., 10012

NON-PROFIT ORG.
U.S. POSTAGE
PAID
NEW YORK, NY
Permit No. 2432

One of the irreverent postcards used by the Tiny Mythic Theater Company in its direct mail fund-raising campaign.

2

THE PERSONAL TOUCH:

"Handwritten" Fund Appeal

CHALLENGE: The end of the San Antonio Symphony's fiscal year was only six weeks away, and more than 300 past donors of $100 to $5,000 still had not renewed their contributions to the annual fund drive.

PLAN: The orchestra's development department thought that a personalized plea to each of the unrenewed donors might make a difference. Elaine Spence, chair of the annual drive, "wrote" 306 handwritten notes—which in actuality were written, addressed and inserted in envelopes by a Minnetonka, Minnesota direct-mail firm, Irresistible Ink, for a cost of under $600. The total cost of the campaign—including note cards printed for fifteen cents each, the use of first-class commemorative stamps on each envelope and follow-up activity—was under $1,000.

RESULT: Within six weeks of the mailing 101 donors sent in contributions. A follow-up phone campaign added another 157 renewals. Overall, 84% of the respondents renewed, with nearly one-third increasing their support over the previous year. A total of $104,000 was raised, which—combined with other activities—enabled the orchestra to close a $300,000 budget gap and finish its season in the black for the first time in ten years. An interesting sidelight to the campaign was the fact that many orchestra supporters took the time to thank Ms. Spence for her incredible work as chair of the annual fund drive. How, they wondered, did she ever find the time to write hundreds of personal letters to prospective donors?

3

First-Timers Become Donors:

Netting Contributors Quickly

CHALLENGE: First-time program attendees also are potential donors. The Strand-Capitol Performing Arts Center in York, Pennsylvania, wanted to turn new ticket-buyers into new supporters as quickly as possible.

PLAN: Striking while the iron is still hot, the Center—using its computer—draws up a list of all first-time attendees. Within a month of the event attended, the Center sends each of them a friendly letter, signed by the membership chair, which thanks them for coming, outlines the benefits and invites them to become contributing members.

RESULT: The results have been well worth the effort. Anywhere from one to ten percent of first-time audience members join the Center within several months, depending on the program attended.

4

Laughing All the Way to the Bank:

Rewarding Donors with Jokes

CHALLENGE: Humor is often used as a means of wooing donors—but how often is it used to reward donors? Mobius, an artist-run center for experimental programs in all areas of the arts, faced bleak funding prospects, with an economic recession in full swing and the mood in Massachusetts generally grim. Yet Mobius, a Boston group that prided itself on being in tune with the times, had a tradition of sending humorous fundraising letters to its supporters. In this kind of climate, wondered its leaders, should it consider the type of funny letter that their donors usually expected?

PLAN: At a board brainstorming session, an interesting idea surfaced: Without including jokes in its fundraising letter—facing the recession head-on—the artist-run center would cheer up its depressed donors by offering them "a joke a week for every ten dollars you contribute." "The recession is no joke," the fundraiser letter said, going on to indicate that while the letter wouldn't have any jokes in it, "despite what you've come to expect from us," a team of experts was working to resolve the humor deficit

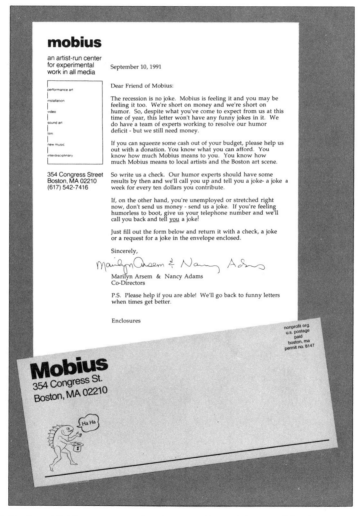

This letter from Mobius to prospective donors makes a joke out of fund-raising.

and would have some results by the time the donor sent in a check. There was even concern voiced for the unemployed or tapped out (who were told, "Don't send us money—send us a joke") and for those feeling humorless (who, it was suggested, could "give us your telephone number and we'll call you back and tell *you* a joke.") Enclosed with each letter was a response envelope with "Ha ha" printed on its face and a form allowing donors to indicate the type of joke they wanted to hear, ranging from insider arts jokes to tasteless jokes to lawyer jokes. One of the topics included on the sheet, "dirty jokes," was crossed out, with a footnote indicating "Oops! We can't tell dirty jokes. We signed the NEA decency clause." Boxes at the bottom of the form were included for those who wanted to send jokes rather than cash, and for the broke and humorless, who could ask to be called with a joke.

RESULT: The letter was one of the most successful in Mobius history, with responses bringing in $4,357 within four months. Of the 128 responses received, 106 included donations ranging from $5 to $1,000, averaging $41.10. The twenty-two other respondents didn't send money, but did send letters or jokes. The campaign also attracted a good deal of attention and, for a brief time in a somber period, helped to cheer up a lot of people.

5

SHIFTING GEARS:

Deferred-Giving Program

CHALLENGE: Celebrating its 25th anniversary, the San Diego Opera seemed poised to launch a successful endowment campaign. Four years of balanced budgets, a cash reserve, a long-range plan that projected artistic growth and financial stability, and a feasibility study that showed the opera could raise six million dollars in cash towards an endowment while *continuing* its three-million-dollar annual campaign, provided good reasons for optimism. However, as the quiet phase of the campaign was progressing—and before a public launching was announced—the economic climate took a turn for the worse. Despite having raised over one million dollars toward the endowment, the opera management recognized that it would be almost impossible under the circumstances to meet the cash goal. With major funding needed to help support the opera company's six-million-dollar annual budget, it was clear that aggressive action had to be taken to find endowment funds.

PLAN: Recognizing that the endowment campaign might jeopardize donations to its annual fund, the opera company dropped its plans for a cash-based endowment and began to tool up for a major new effort—an all-out deferred-giving program. Following an eighteen-month planning process, which involved major research, the preparation of materials designed to encompass a range of deferred-giving options, and donor identification, the company launched its renamed "Opera Stars" program. Campaign chair Esther J. Burnham accepted a board challenge—an offer of $125,000 in cash reserve funds, to be placed in a new endowment trust if she could raise an additional $125,000 in cash. Within three months, she raised that amount and also brought in several major deferred gifts.

The public phase of the new program was initiated with a mailing to all subscribers and members—6,500 households—outlining the Opera Stars program and its various membership options: gifts of life insurance, bequests, charitable remainder unitrusts and pooled income funds. Ensuing complimentary "Smart Gifts" seminars, conducted by a nationally known speaker, focused on ways that donors could benefit themselves and the opera company through deferred and planned giving, and offered attendees gift certificates or free attendance at a performance. Virtually every informational and promotional material produced by the opera company—from programs to magazines to ticket wallets mailed to subscribers—included data on Opera Stars. For dramatic effect, the company used "teaser slides" above its supertitles before performances, inviting attendees to turn to a page in the program which included Opera Stars information and names of members.

RESULT: In its first eighteen months, the San Diego Opera raised seven-and-a-half million dollars for the Opera Stars program. There have been no signs of let-up since, as the program continues on a year-round basis. The special promotional and informational programs have been very successful, with the use of supertitles in one instance spurring an audience member to phone the opera company days afterwards and arrange a meeting, resulting weeks later in a $500,000 charitable reminder unitrust gift.

6

IN THE NAME OF THE DONOR:

Relating a Name Campaign to Activity

CHALLENGE: Arts fund-raisers seldom miss the opportunity to win contributions by offering donors a named site in return for their gift: concert hall seats, staircases and entire buildings all have been offered and accepted. Faced with the need to win support for a new exhibit area with interactive multimedia in a facility soon to be constructed, the Museum of Paleontology at the University of California, Berkeley, was looking for a funding concept that would relate to its primary area of activity.

PLAN: Looking at naming opportunities that had been utilized successfully by other groups, the museum decided on a concept with which they could clearly identify—

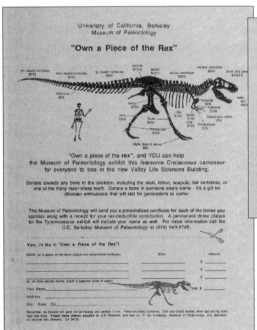

A Museum of Paleontology donor appeal to name a dinosaur part.

dinosaur bones. Specifically, the museum announced, in a promotional campaign that it would be assembling a *Tyrannosaurus rex* for its new display and that donors would have the opportunity to have their names identified with a specific dinosaur part, from a chevron tail bone at $20 to teeth at $256 each, from ribs at $150 all the way up to the pelvis at $2500 and the skull and jaws at $5000. Prospective donors, reached by direct mail, advertising and fliers distributed at key sites in the university and elsewhere, were wooed with the promise that their names would appear on a permanent plaque mounted near the 300-piece dinosaur, and that they would be invited to an open house for all donors.

RESULT: Within months, the campaign raised $9,000, with the promise of much more to come (especially since dinosaur teeth are replaceable and can be sold again and again). The press also responded, and publicity included a feature in the *New York Times.*

7

Your Membership Card is Waiting:

Upgrading Members

CHALLENGE: Among the thousands of concertgoers drawn every summer to Wolf Trap's season of performing arts at the Filene Center, just outside of Washington, DC, were many who had never contributed plus current contributors whose donations as members of the Wolf Trap Associates were in the lowest ($50) membership category. Recognizing an opportunity to attract new members and upgrade existing members, the Wolf Trap Foundation's development and membership staffs decided that the time was ripe for a new approach to its annual direct-mail campaign.

PLAN: A list of 65,000 names was selected for the new-donor acquisition campaign, focusing on zip codes from the greater Washington, DC area. Launched November first, with subsequent mail drops (for a total of three solicitations) through late January, the campaign emphasized such membership benefits as early ordering privileges, designated parking and event invitations, and drew on information about each recipient's past attendance at Wolf Trap. While not excluding basic $50 memberships, the $100 and higher categories were emphasized. Different teaser lines were used for each mailing, on both the outside envelope and in each letter. One cover line read, "The days are growing shorter...and so is your time to make the most of Wolf Trap next year." The renewal campaign, launched at the same time but running through the following April, consisted of five solicitations, each also emphasizing the benefits of membership, but suggesting renewals in the higher categories. Among the different envelope tag lines used were, "Make sure there's music in the air again next year. Renew your membership now." followed by "Our schedule is about to be mailed. Your check should be too," ending with "Silent Summer?"

RESULT: The more expensive acquisition campaign, with direct costs of $79,000, was successful, resulting in revenues of $110,000. The renewal campaign, with costs of only $22,000, brought in $350,000 in income as a result of a renewal rate of nearly 65%. Significantly, the conversion rate to a higher membership category was an estimated 75%.

8

MEMBERSHIP RENEWAL:

Visual Reminder Concept

CHALLENGE: The Strand-Capitol Performing Arts Center in York, Pennsylvania was seeking an effective way of getting members to renew, even after they ignored the initial reminder.

PLAN: The Arts Center developed a renewal-reminder series, beginning with a first mailing which showed a wide-open curtain. Each subsequent reminder showed the curtain closed a little more than in the previous mailer. The fourth and last reminder showed the curtain closed completely. For added visual effect, a troupe of jugglers, featured on each cover, drops a progressively larger number of clubs with each reminder. When all had failed, and it looked like "curtains" for the Center, members received a handwritten note from the membership chair, reminding them of the need for their support and urging them to renew their membership.

RESULT: Since introducing this strategy, the Center has upped its renewal rate to about 90% of its 3,000+ members. The progressive reminders have been effective, producing results on an approximate 40-30-20 ratio for each successive mailing.

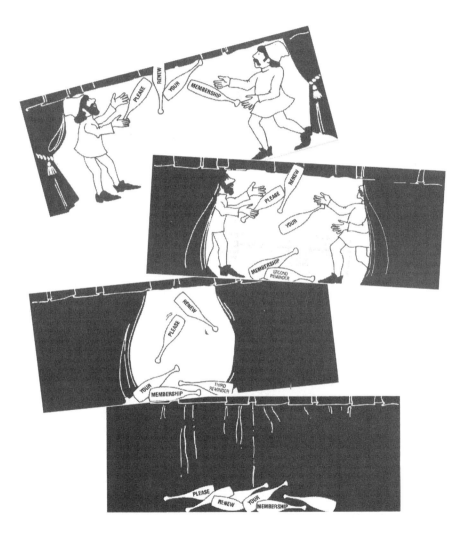

The Strand-Capitol Performing Arts Center's renewal reminder series of mailings.

9

MAKING THE TOP TEN:

Adapting a Concept from TV

CHALLENGE: The Ulster Performing Arts Center (UPAC) in Kingston, New York was looking for a new direct-mail funding approach to give a major boost to raising its $500,000 budget. The previous year's mailing had raised only $6,000, and development director Jon Wojciechowski thought that an eye-catching, attention-getting concept—humorous without being offensive—was needed. Why not borrow and reshape an idea, he thought, that was familiar to television audiences: comedian David Letterman's "Top Ten List"? (In one of the more popular features of his nightly network-TV show, Letterman reads a list that offers ten funny reasons to explain such concerns as "why your local news team is dumb.")

PLAN: Although the Center president was skeptical, a positive reaction by other board members convinced him that "Top 10 Reasons To Support UPAC" was worth a try. The mailer, desktop-published by Wojciechowski, was a modest and inexpensive piece which cost $270 to print and $700 to mail to 4,000 names on the Center's list—many of them past donors. The piece blended humorous and serious reasons for supporting the Center, beginning with number 10, "Only opportunity to see two socialites fight over the last bag of Skittles," ending with the top or number one reason, "Without your generosity and support, UPAC would disappear."

RESULT: Nearly $20,000—more than triple the previous year—was raised. Many donors took the time to say how much they enjoyed the mailer, including some who said they hadn't given in the past but had decided to donate now because of this approach.

TOP 10 REASONS TO SUPPORT UPAC

10. Only opportunity to see socialites fight over the last bag of skittles.

9. All the obnoxious teens are at the movies.

8. The dimly lit balcony. *(Need we say more?)*

7. Making congress debate over arts appropriations keeps them out of trouble.

6. No complicated remote control to fiddle with. We do all the work.

5. Chance to see real actors sweat for their salary — not like those spoiled movie stars.

4. It would make a lousy parking lot.

3. Save money. No taxes on show tickets.

2. Exclusive guarantee: You won't see the Energizer Rabbit even once during a performance.

The Ulster Performing Arts Center's "Top Ten" fund-raising mailing.

1. Without your generousity and support, UPAC would disappear.

Although many more exciting events are scheduled throughout the summer, the 1991-92 Subscription Season has come to an end. This past season was one of remarkable progress, and UPAC has launched itself forward into the future.

Your generosity last season gave us new carpeting, fire doors, stage riffing and restored front portico and facade. It provided for a new roof over our offices and helped remodel our box office. Other happenings include free parking in the national micronetics parking lot, and free shuttle bus service from the lot to the theatre. This past winter, The Studio at UPAC began offering training for students age 6 to adult in acting, dance, voice and more.

That's the good news, The bad news is that government funding is at a all-time low. Foundation and grants are drying up because of the poor economics conditions, and the recession has hurt many contributors. UPAC ticket sales now cover approximately 40 percent of our annual expenses; the remaining 60 percent comes from these dwindling sources.

So, again, we turn to you for financial help. Your support is more important now than ever before.

Please consider mailing back your contribution in the enclosed envelope today. And thank you for helping to keep this beautiful theatre alive and active.

10

STRINGS ATTACHED:

Eye-Catching Mailer

CHALLENGE: The development staff at the Phoenix Symphony was looking for a new mailing piece that could serve both for renewals and acquisitions. Afraid that a typical fund-raising appeal letter would be boring to the recipients, they wanted to introduce a piece which would have immediate eye-catching appeal.

PLAN: Someone in the development office recalled that several years earlier a concert sponsor, Linda Brock Automotive, had used a cut-out violin as a program stuffer to invite concertgoers and musicians to a post-performance reception. Why not adapt the violin, with an appropriate message inside it, to the fund-raising needs of the orchestra? The automotive company gave the original dye cut to the orchestra, which printed up thousands with a special message inside. When the violin was opened, one of its two sides read, "A Violin Without a Bow is Like the Phoenix Symphony Without You." The other side, reading "I want to play my part," was a contribution card with suggested gifts of $25, $50, $100 and Other.

RESULT: Introduced in mid-season, the piece proved very successful. Although official records weren't available because of staff changes, Gail Warden, the symphony's development director at the time, recalls that the orchestra had excellent results with the piece, attracting a good deal of attention and a significant number of new donors. "We used it both as a direct mail piece and program stuffer over several seasons," she said. "In fact, we used it so much that we had to make a new dye cut." The greatest inroad was in donations from concertgoers who normally did not contribute.

11

ADOPT, DON'T ADAPT:

Donors Adopt Characters from Plays

CHALLENGE: Shakespeare on Wheels, a free, traveling summer theatre program of the University of Maryland, Baltimore County, was expanding. Due to a growing demand for its services, the budget, normally about $75,000, had jumped to $130,000 for the tenth anniversary season, and staff and student participation had grown. Several years earlier, an endowment fund had been established to support the program; now, for the first time, modest interest income of about $1,300 was available. While support from the state arts council had doubled to $12,000, corporate solicitations had not been successful and, clearly, additional income was needed.

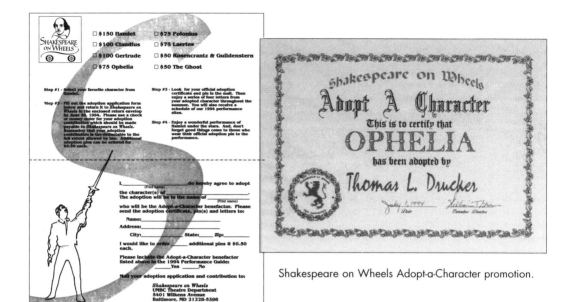

Shakespeare on Wheels Adopt-a-Character promotion.

PLAN: William T. Brown, the company's founder and executive producer, reacted to a suggestion from his board chair, Donna Singleton Burke, who noted that such programs as "adopt a highway" or "adopt a sculpture" had been successful. He thought the concept might be adaptable for his theatre. Precedent was on his side in the arts, in fact, since several such programs had already been introduced, including the Orchestra of Illinois's program that had invited audience members to adopt the musician of their choice at prices ranging from $250 up to $1,000 (for the conductor).

Shakespeare on Wheels introduced its "Adopt-a-Character" campaign by inviting some 10,000 direct-mail recipients to select one of eight characters: $150 for Hamlet; $100 for either Claudius or Gertrude; $75 for Ophelia, Polonius or Laertes; and $50 for a paired Rosencrantz and Guildenstern or for the ghost. Adopters were promised a personalized certificate of adoption, an adoption button featuring the name of the adopted character and a series of four letters during the summer season, "written to you from the perspective of your character." Donors attending performances were invited to wear their button and meet their "offspring" at the end of the performance. Additionally, all adopters received an autographed cast photo at the end of the season, and early adopters received tenth-anniversary T-shirts.

RESULT: The Adopt-a-Character concept, now an annual Shakespeare on Wheels program, helped call attention to the company's funding need, and attracted notice throughout the state. Donors also commended the theatre on its personal involvement with their characters. Importantly, it met is $10,000 funding goal.

12

ONLY TEN LOUSY BUCKS:

Direct Pitch for Small Contributions

CHALLENGE: Moving into its own theatre, the Manhattan Class Company in New York City needed an instant flux of funds to help pay for needed renovations. An advisory board member came up with an interesting suggestion. Why not ask audiences for only $10? After all, how could anyone possibly object to giving only "ten lousy bucks"?

PLAN: The staff jumped on the idea and developed a letter, using humor as the lever to pry dollars from donors. The letter, which opened with a straightforward request, "Please send us ten dollars," went on to list specific reasons, from plain and simple to lofty, philosophical, personal and historic, to justify why "Specifically, what we ask of you is TEN * LOUSY * BUCKS!" The following paragraph indicated that if respondents took out the "ten lousy bucks" now ("more would be great,") and put the money in the pre-addressed envelope with the reply card, they'd probably not even miss the $10. Hand-addressed by volunteers, the letters were mailed after the close of the season to all ticket buyers from the previous three seasons who were not already donors, and to current donors as well.

RESULT: The response was immediate and excellent, with about $15,000 raised from the mailing. In fact, the theatre staff was so pleased that it decided to use the same letter again, but only to non-donors, every year. The results have continued to be excellent. The most recent mailing, with a response rate of five percent and an average donation of $39, exceeded the theatre's goal.

Chapter Eight

Fund-Raising Events and Concepts

1

ARTISTIC FUND-RAISER:

Tying Funding Event to Artistic Concept

CHALLENGE: Artists Space, a New York City group which provides both exhibition opportunities and financial help to emerging and mid-career artists, was looking for a fund-raising event to reach a difficult dual goal: to raise a good deal of money and to relate to the organization's artistic concept.

PLAN: Ken Buhler, the organization's technical director, turned his enthusiasm for miniature golf into a major artistic concept. The fund-raising event that emerged was "Putt-Modernism," a playable 18-hole miniature golf course with each hole designed by a different prominent artist (among them Cindy Sherman, Elizabeth Murray and Gregory Amenoff). As envisioned, the resulting work would be both art and popular culture.

RESULT: The combination exhibition/sporting event/fund-raiser at the Artists Space gallery turned into a veritable goldmine during its initial two-month run, earning $85,000 for the arts organization. It drew some 20,000 people, paying $5 each to play the course, and an additional 10,000 attendees—many of them first-time Artists Space visitors—who came to see the exhibition and watch the players. It also won sponsorship from the Philip Morris Companies. The following year, the exhibition was remodeled slightly and had a second run in New York City, which was followed by a two-year national tour of six cities, plus a return visit to New York, earning even more money for the organization along with tremendous national and international visibility.

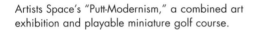

Artists Space's "Putt-Modernism," a combined art exhibition and playable miniature golf course.

2

CHILD'S PLAY:

Building Funding Event Around a Celebrity

CHALLENGE: Sometimes a proven success is worth repeating, if a way can be found to make it look fresh and different. The Long Wharf Theatre in New Haven, Connecticut initiated a series of annual spring fund-raising events by saluting the noted celebrity chef in "Julia Child Onstage," followed by a "Salute to Arthur Miller" the next year and "Brown Goes Silver" the year after that, a celebration of Arvin Brown's twenty-fifth year as artistic director of Long Wharf. When discussion of a fourth event for the following year got underway, Ms. Child was suggested again because of her tremendous popularity and the success of the first event. However, since a different kind of event was needed to attract attention, the theatre staff decided to shape a unique three-day extravaganza around Ms. Child, featuring a gala dinner with her, a silent auction and two onstage cooking demonstrations by the television chef. With Ms. Child's approval, planning commenced for the event.

PLAN: Since the event, now titled "Picnic in Provence With Julia Child," would focus on Ms. Child's unrivaled culinary skills, it was important to involve food experts in the planning. Following initial discussions with potential sponsors, the theatre organized a benefit committee of key Long Wharf volunteers and an advisory committee drawn from Connecticut's culinary community. The latter group served as event resources, helping to find gifts for the silent auction, promoting the event in their publications, restaurants or offices, and opening doors for Long Wharf to approach other potential suppliers of goods and services. The working benefit committee followed up on every lead and helped shape the event by determining everything from ticket prices to decor, from auction items to invitations and promotional pieces. As the event grew in complexity, 167 volunteers as well as staff members became involved in such tasks as transforming the theatre into a virtual restaurant and the lobbies into decorated entrance halls in the style of southern France, and assembling all the materials needed to construct sets for the cooking demonstrations. The event that emerged from the planning featured an opening night program with a cocktail reception and the silent auction of contributed food-related items (including such elegant entries as a private wine reception for twenty-five at Chamard Vineyards), followed by the "picnic" with Ms. Child in the theatre's second-stage space and its scene shop, with food contributed by a local restaurant. Attendees paid $175 for the complete evening or $50 for the reception and auction. On the following two days, donors could attend Ms. Child's onstage cooking demonstrations for $35. To lend a festive air to the event and distinguish it from past black-tie fundraisers, the suggested attire was "picnic chic or summer white."

A flier for the Long Wharf Theatre's "Picnic in Provence With Julia Child."

RESULT: Because of its precision-like planning, the event came off without a hitch. In addition to the contributed auction prizes and food, and Ms. Child's contribution of her time, sponsors were found for the gala picnic and cooking demonstrations. The event, which generated tremendous good will for the theatre, had other virtues as well. With expenses for the mammoth undertaking less than $40,000 (and many items donated), it turned out to be quite a sumptuous picnic, netting $106,066 for the theatre.

3

BLACK LEATHER PAS DE DEUX:

Informal Social Event

CHALLENGE: When planning for its annual fund-raiser was in the initial stages, the Royal Winnipeg Ballet had four key goals: to raise the budgeted figure to $50,000 ($2,000 higher than the previous year); to depart completely in theme and concept from the previous year's major fund-raising event, a movie premiere; to dispel the myth that ballet is only for the elite; and to attract affluent urban professionals who had no previous involvement with the ballet.

PLAN: A board member—a friend of the president of Harley-Davidson Canada—knew that the motorcycle company had had great success in marketing to an audience sought by the ballet: affluent urban professionals in their forties and fifties. When she casually suggested that his company might sponsor a ballet benefit and he seemed agreeable, she recommended a "biker party" to a very responsive board. In its preliminary planning, the event committee—composed of three board members and seven younger community-oriented people—agreed initially on tone and climate. The event had to be social, informal, mobile and danceable. Before formally asking Harley-Davidson for its support, the committee also agreed that a show of Harley-Davidson-licensed fashions should be a key part of the event.

After working out a plan for the party in all its aspects, the committee met with Harley-Davidson staff people and reached agreement on several points: Harley-Davidson would supply clothing for the fashion show; they would make a "Heritage

Softail Classic" motorcycle available at wholesale cost for a raffle (normally there's a two-year wait for purchasers of this popular model); and they would co-sponsor the event. Although the ballet company suggested a $10,000 donation from the cycle company for its role as sponsor, Harley-Davidson recommended a co-sponsorship, putting up $5,000 and helping the dance company find another $5,000 co-sponsor. The dance company also found additional and unexpected help when a board member was able to find them a rent-free airplane hangar at Winnipeg International Airport as the party site.

RESULT: The party was a rousing social and financial success which also reaped tremendous publicity. It included demonstration bike rides by Harley owners, bike displays, a tattoo parlor with removable tattoos, dancing, and the hi-tech, multilevel-stage fashion show ending with the sweepstakes drawing. Some 400 people attended, including 140 who had no previous association with the ballet. Each guest received a free souvenir poster, the designers of which, according to the staff, "thought the concept was so cool that they donated it." Tickets at $100 each included one raffle chance, and additional lottery tickets were sold at $20 each or three for $50. Overall, the dance company netted $55,000—$15,000 from the event and a much-higher-than-anticipated $40,000 from the raffle. "The people attending had a blast," said director of development Jane Corbett. "We also won the kind of press coverage— national as well as local—that you don't usually get with your dance programs."

4

MILKING THE DONOR:

Funding Event Tied in to Local Setting

CHALLENGE: The Kamloops Art Gallery in British Columbia, Canada, was looking for a unique fund-raiser that would tie in to its location in prime ranching and cattle country, an area where livestock is as much a part of the scenery as mountains and deserts are. When a board member saw miniature black-and-white ceramic banks in the shape of cows at a trade show in Vancouver, she knew that the perfect funding vehicle was at hand.

PLAN: A proposal was presented to the board. The Gallery would purchase 1,500 of the cows at the wholesale price of $5 each, put them on display in a grass lot and resell them to donors for $10 each. The board, sold on the idea, committed itself to a cash outlay of $7,500 for the purchase of the cows and additional funds for shipping, storage and promotional purposes. Part of the extra funds, about $1,500 overall, was used to purchase cow t-shirts that were included with press kits sent to journalists.

RESULT: With the help of local business and the entire board (which camped out to guard the herd of 1,500 cows on the night before the event took place), the cattle sale (dubbed "Until the Cows Go Home") became a community cause célèbre and a financial success as well. Petro-Canada loaned a field convenient to main roads for display of the cows and also made a donation to the Gallery of two cents for every liter of gas sold on the Saturday and Sunday that the event was held. Also, a dairy provided black-and-white ice cream, a bakery made cow cookies and a barbershop offered prizes for cowlicks. Press coverage was widespread, with newspaper headlines including such puns and jokes as "The Gallery is milking the event." Mail-order sales came in inadvertently when a Vancouver news program showed the cows on live TV prior to the event. When the actual event was held there was sales mayhem—all the cows were sold within forty-eight hours. Responding to the demand, the Gallery gift shop ordered 2,000 more, all of which were sold as well. Overall, the gallery not only netted over $15,000, but involved its local community and won tremendous publicity as well.

The Kamloops Art Gallery's field of ceramic cows, offered for sale.

5

PASS THE PLATE:

Churches Raise Funds for Theatre

CHALLENGE: The Crossroads Theatre Company, America's largest theatre focusing on the production and promotion of African-American theatre, was seeking a new way to win support from its primary target audience.

PLAN: Because African-American churchgoers are noted for their generosity, the theatre turned to area churches for support. The Reverend Buster Soaries, a longtime theatre supporter, organized a "Crossroads Clergy Committee," which invited area churches to host a "Crossroads Theatre Sunday," during which they would pass the plate not only for themselves, but for the theatre as well.

RESULT: Seven local churches participated in the first "Crossroads Theatre Sunday." Although the amount of money raised was quite modest, the promotion helped foster a new working relationship between the theatre and area churches, which resulted in church groups buying what theatre development director Mercia Weyand called "a lot of tickets" for Crossroads productions. Also, additional plate-passing Sundays were organized.

6

MAKING AN ART OUT OF A DRAWING:

Getting Raffle Prize Donated

CHALLENGE: When planning for the Studio Arena Theatre's annual benefit auction was underway, the development staff started looking for an extra funding feature that could help boost proceeds by an additional $5,000. After studying various options, the development staff decided that a raffle was its best bet and that a car was the one item that would have universal appeal. Because raffles were illegal for nonprofit corporations in New York State, the theatre—on the advice of counsel—decided to have a "drawing," with tickets for the drawing exchanged for $10 donations.

PLAN: The initial task facing the theatre was to find an automobile dealer who would be willing to donate a car or make one available at a very substantial discount. When the local Jeep/Eagle Dealers' Association expressed some interest but wanted substantial exposure in return—the kind that the theatre alone couldn't provide—the theatre did what any clever arts group in the same situation would do: It called in a third party that could provide the exposure and help itself at the same time. The third party was the local television station, Adelphia Cable, where—fortuitously—the marketing director had a personal relationship with a member of the theatre's staff. Adelphia agreed to provide the Dealers' Association with TV advertising valued at $100,000, over the course of the year; the Association agreed to donate a Jeep to the theatre for the drawing and to place a Jeep in the Studio Arena lobby for the entire season; Studio Arena, in turn, agreed to acknowledge both Adelphia Cable and the Dealers' Association in all its printed materials and in a banner hung over the box office, to provide each with all of the benefits given to corporate donors at the $10,000 and higher level, and to pay Adelphia Cable $4,000 for the cost of advertising the drawing on television. Drawing tickets (an in-kind donation from a local printer) were sold by ushers at each theatre performance—with incentives provided for selling the most tickets—and the board and other volunteers were given ten tickets each to sell. The Jeep, parked in the lobby, helped give the promotional boost to the effort.

RESULT: The results far exceeded expectations. With usher sales leading the way, the modest funding goal of $5,000 was easily surpassed and the theatre grossed $36,100. With its only expense the $4,000 for television advertising costs, the net amount was a healthy $32,100. Another Jeep drawing with the same participants was held the following year; the amount raised was nearly the same—$30,780 net—although the reaction to the Jeep in the theatre lobby was quite different, with some patrons questioning whether the Jeep had ever really been given away in the first place, since this could have been the same vehicle. The theatre responded by placing on the Jeep pictures of the winner holding her prize ticket. Moral: As many arts administrators know, things are seldom the same the second time around.

7

TIME FOR A BREAK:

New Look for Old Event

CHALLENGE: When an annual fund-raising event proves popular, the temptation might be to repeat it year after year. As many arts groups have discovered, however, donors often tire of the same event, and unless a hiatus is taken the event can wear out its welcome. The Asheville, North Carolina Art Museum faced this situation following its fourth Raffle Party. Initiated as a board fund-raiser, the evening with food and open bar featured a raffle of three works of art, each valued at several thousand dollars or more. To increase the odds of winning, sales were limited to 300 tickets at $100 each. Although the most recent raffle was successful—netting $8,069—the board felt that a change was needed because some members were tiring of the event.

PLAN: For the next three years, the board held different kinds of fund-raising events, including theme parties. Then the board felt that it was time to go back to the raffle, giving it a new look, more sparkle and a different name. Thus, Museum Lotto was born. Held in conjunction with the opening of an exhibition of glass by Louis Comfort Tiffany, "Tiffany Gold," the event—priced at $125 for two attendees—included refreshments and an exhibition lecture by the guest curator. Raffle ticket sales for the three works offered—including a Tiffany vase—were limited to 200, increasing the odds of winning.

RESULT: Led by an aggressive board effort, with some members selling 20 tickets or more, Museum Lotto was successful, netting $8,850, drawing a number of fresh faces and winning many compliments.

$\underline{\overline{8}}$

SOMETHING IN RETURN:

The Right Site

CHALLENGE: Dancing in the Streets, an organization that has pioneered in the use of everyday spaces as performance venues—from warehouses to railroad terminals to housing projects—was celebrating its tenth anniversary. Several months prior to the time tentatively set aside for an anniversary fund-raiser, executive director Elise Bernhardt was asked by Anita Contini, the director of the arts and events program at the World Financial Center in Manhattan, whether her group might curate a program for the Center's spring performance series. Needing an exciting site for her fund-raiser, Bernhardt decided to ask for something in return for curating the series, in addition to a fee: use of the World Financial Center's famed Winter Garden for the tenth anniversary Dancing in the Streets fund-raising gala.

PLAN: An agreement was reached quickly. Dancing in the Streets would curate a four-week series, open to the public without charge, for a small fee. The final event of the series would combine the performance with a buffet reception for Dancing's benefit guests at Sfuzzi, a restaurant immediately adjacent to the performance space. Dancing in the Streets, which would pay for the reception at a slightly reduced rate, also would have 150 reserved seats for its guests in the Winter Garden for the public performance and for the "dancing under the palms" that followed.

Dancing in the Street's fund-raising gala at the World Financial Center.

RESULT: The gala, which netted $10,000, was the most successful fund-raiser ever held by Dancing in the Streets. "By being attached to a series at the World Financial Center, we had a setting we otherwise couldn't have obtained," observed Ms. Bernhardt. "Also, by having a public audience of 1,500 people for the performance, we were able to show our benefit guests what we were doing." Helped by its setting and the relatively low price for a benefit—tickets were $100 each; $50 for artists—the event attracted many new potential supporters among the 235 paid attendees. To entertain her clients, one board member alone bought 75 tickets.

9

WHEN FUNDING'S A PIECE OF CAKE:

Promotions Revive Fund Drive

CHALLENGE: The fifty-five million dollar capital campaign to fund construction of the new Raymond F. Kravis Center for the Performing Arts in Palm Beach, Florida, had been on hold, awaiting the appointment of the Center's new executive director. With the official opening only a few years away, a newly-hired executive team on board, and more than half the money still to be raised, the time for a major promotional drive to revive the lagging funding effort was clearly at hand.

PLAN: Through staff brainstorming sessions led by new executive director, Arnold Breman, plans for a high-intensity drive were developed. Designed to create excitement and capture the attention of both the general public and the local business and tourism community, to boost the fund drive and to broaden interest in the Center's tourism potential, the concept envisioned was a series of promotions throughout the several years leading up to the center's official opening. Held roughly once a month, the events included such attention-getters as a conductor leading a full symphony orchestra in a musical tribute to the pouring of the Center's first concrete; a parade of 2,000 people through the construction site to the strains of the "Triumphal March" from Verdi's *Aïda*; a cement mixer-truck emblazoned with a slogan to "get mixed up with the Center"; and a "hard-hat concert" for construction workers. Seeking an event that would have county-wide impact, the Center asked the Publix Super Market chain if it would bake a giant cake in the shape of the Center and tour it to its stores throughout the area; the resulting 150-pound cake's well-publicized tour was highlighted in some instances by opening ceremonies involving local business and tourism leaders, and the cake was accompanied wherever it went by brochures giving information on the new facility and soliciting small donations from grassroots donors.

RESULT: The events achieved their purpose by attracting considerable public and media attention and making virtually the entire county aware of the upcoming opening of the new facility. The campaign also helped put the Center's funding drive back on course and, while the events themselves were not designed as major funding efforts, they attracted contributions from many small donors, including $7,000 raised from the cake tour. By the time the Center opened, it had met its multimillion-dollar funding goal.

10

WHEN OPPORTUNITY KNOCKS:

Estate Auctions

CHALLENGE: The New Jersey State Opera Guild was presented with an interesting funding opportunity: A New Jersey company that conducted estate auctions, State Auction Liquidators, offered to make the opera company a beneficiary of an upcoming auction of a mansion's contents—it could collect all of the auction admission fees—if the Guild would give its mailing list to the auctioneer to help attract bidders.

PLAN: The Guild was quick to respond to the offer, setting the admission fee at a modest $5. State Auction Liquidators, in turn, mailed fliers announcing the on-site auction in support of the New Jersey State Opera to the entire Guild mailing list, and placed newspaper ads indicating that the $5 admission fee would be donated to the opera company. The Opera Guild talked up the event to its members.

RESULT: The auction went so well that State Auction Liquidators made the opera company the beneficiary of three more auctions during the season. Without much effort, the New Jersey State Opera Guild raised over $10,000 for the opera company from admission fees for the four auctions.

11

TOWN CELEBRITY:

Recognition Days for Donors

CHALLENGE: An arts center in a small community doesn't have the resources for major fund drives and often can be most successful if it can tie local involvement into its funding effort. Recognizing the need for an ongoing approach that would achieve this, the board and staff of the Orangeburg, South Carolina Arts Center kicked around a number of ideas before board member Lois Lusty came up with a concept that seemed just right for Orangeburg.

PLAN: The Arts Center initiated the "365 Club," with membership open to anyone in the community. For a $50 contribution, donors can have special recognition for themselves or anyone they designate on the day of their choice. The name of the person to be recognized is mounted on a large poster and set on an easel in the Arts Center lobby, where it remains throughout the day. Above the poster is a giant calendar listing every day of the year. All new Club members receive written notes and phone calls from the Center, thanking them for "making our day," and they're listed in the organization newsletter as well.

RESULT: The concept has been popular since its inception, with about half the days sold each year for such occasions as birthdays, anniversaries, memorials or any special event. The Arts Center nets over $6,000 a year from the Club, or about 6% of its annual budget. The Club also has been a good promotional vehicle, which has helped draw visitors inside the Center's door.

12

Donor Happy Hour:

In-house Benefit

CHALLENGE: Many major donors to San Diego's Old Globe Theatre attend performances regularly. The theatre was looking for a way to provide some extra benefit to Circle Patron members—donors of $1,000 or more annually—when they attended performances.

PLAN: The Old Globe gives all Circle Patron members twelve "Bard Cards": coupons good for one complimentary beverage at the theatre's bar or concession stand.

RESULT: At a redemption cost of only $1 each, the theatre found an easy and renewable way to thank their key donors. The theatre distributes some 2,400 cards each year and also uses them as special donation incentives during its telefunding campaigns.

This coupon good for one complimentary
beverage at the Bar or Concession Stand

Valid through 10/94

The Old Globe Theatre's Bard Card for Circle Patron members.

13

Don't Change Partners:

Fun for Younger Volunteers

CHALLENGE: To get the most out of their volunteers, arts groups must find ways to involve them in a range of activities that are interesting and personally rewarding, and which reap positive results for the organization. For younger volunteers—those under or close to forty years old—another ingredient must often be added to the mix—fun. When a governing board of nine founding members formed the Playhouse Square Partners for Cleveland's giant theatre restoration project, Playhouse Square Center, they recognized the need to wrap the Partners in a mantle of fun and excitement if it was to attract additional members.

PLAN: With great media fanfare (and a working group of fifty-two "Premiere Partners") Playhouse Square Partners was formally launched at a cocktail party at the Palace Theatre that attracted a turn-away crowd of 500. Within two weeks, eighty-five new Partners, contributing anywhere from $50 to $1000 (with appropriate benefits at each level), joined the group. The image of Partners as an active, lively, involved force was helped immeasurably by its first annual Jump Back Ball, an engaging affair that attracted 421 people, raised nearly $7,000 for the Center and was named "Benefit of the Year" by *Northern Ohio Live Magazine*. Subsequent Balls have been equally adventurous and unpredictable, including an affair with the theme "Spy vs. Spy," which opened with the Cleveland Police Department's SWAT team descending from the ceiling into the State Theater Auditorium. Partners defines itself as an arts organization, but one that is not the least bit traditional. As its brochure states, "We love music, plays, entertainment—all wrapped up in a fun and funky, uncommon and unconventional, sometimes irreverent spirit of adventure. From the glitter of the Jump Back Ball to theatre renovation work parties, we're here for the arts, the excitement and each other."

RESULT: Since it was organized, Partners membership has grown each year, and the funds raised through its activities have grown as well. The *Saturday Night Live*-themed Jump Back Ball attracted 595 people and raised $40,000. Thanks to its lively image and the range of its support activities, membership grew from 293 to 397 to 470 members over a three-year period. In that time, Partners raised $165,000 for Playhouse Square.

14

EVERYONE'S AN ARTIST:

Involving Local Leaders

CHALLENGE: When it comes to fund-raising, the arts often take a back seat to other local charities in a small town. In tiny Tryon, North Carolina the Upstairs Gallery (the local museum) needed a funding event that would not only bring in money but would involve local leaders and also provide significant visibility in the community.

PLAN: Stealing a lead from the National Football League's "Pass, Punt and Kick" contest for youngsters, the Gallery held its own version, "Paint, Mess and Stick," with the mayor, a bank president and other local celebrities paying up to $250 each to sit at easels (provided by Upstairs) and become artists for a day. Townspeople paid $10 each to applaud or gently mock the neophytes' efforts. When all the "artists" finished their work everyone went inside the Galley, where the completed work was auctioned off.

RESULT: Because of the involvement of the "celebrities," the event drew tremendous local publicity and was well attended, with many newcomers in the audience. Everyone had a fun time—and over $3,500 was raised.

15

WOOING AND REWARDING MAJOR DONORS:

Winning Medals

CHALLENGE: Arts organizations which must plan their seasons and book their artists years in advance—as opera companies usually do—also need the security of knowing that money will be there when it's needed. Recognizing that a commitment of funding spread over several years might be more attractive to donors than the total amount given up front, the San Diego Opera set out to develop a multi-year funding program that would recognize and reward large donors for their support.

The San Diego Opera's Bravissimo Medal, awarded to major donors.

PLAN: In conjunction with the board, the development department introduced the Bravissimo Medal program. Through the program, the opera solicits gifts in three giving categories: gold medals at $100,000 or higher; silver medals at $50,000 to $99,999; and bronze medals at $25,000 to $49,999. Medalists, who contribute one-fourth of their overall pledge each year for four years, receive special benefits, including recognition in all opera publications and invitations to key events. The medals, awarded in a ceremony at the season-opening gala, are worn throughout the opera season.

RESULT: The medal program has resulted in additional income of $800,000 to $1,000,000 a season, allowing the company to plan future seasons with greater security. In its first six years, the program awarded 88 medals overall—21 gold, 18 silver and 46 bronze. The renewal rate after the four-year commitment has been 70% and 50% of the renewals have moved into higher categories.

Chapter Nine

Other Ways to Make Money

1

THE HAT TRICK:

Licensing Dollars

CHALLENGE: Like many of America's cultural institutions, the American Museum of Natural History in New York City has had major financial concerns in recent years. Although it had relied primarily on philanthropy over the years to support its $50 million annual budget, diminishing government support and a general dropoff in private funding had let it to explore other income options that would be consistent with its missions and goals. One of those options was licensing and product development, an area with which the museum had never had a proactive involvement, such activities, until then, being limited to small publishing ventures and items produced for its gift shop.

PLAN: The development staff started seriously to research the possibility of introducing a major licensing program, focusing on products based on or inspired by its collection that might appeal to a national market. Among the items considered were collections of fabrics, wallpaper and children's merchandise; but—reacting to a consultant's suggestion—the staff decided that a hat associated with the museum's history and mission might be the best product with which to launch the new program. When a search through old photos showed that museum explorers (going all the way back to famed dinosaur hunter Roy Chapman Andrews) had worn a special kind of expedition hat, the museum staff knew it had found its item. It approached Harrison-Hoge Industries, Inc., a company with a solid reputation in direct marketing (and an advertiser of its products in the museum's magazine) to determine its interest in making and marketing the hats under a licensing arrangement. Negotiations lasted six

The American Museum of Natural History's "Expedition Hat" offered for sale through its licensing program.

months and a contract was signed, giving Harrison-Hoge the right to manufacture and market the Expedition Hat, as it became known, with the museum receiving an advance against 10% royalty for each hat sold. Within two months of the signing, the direct-mail sales campaign for the hats, retailing at $30 each, was launched by Harrison-Hoge, boosted by ads in such publications as the *Atlantic Monthly*, the *New York Times* and a number of other large-city newspapers.

RESULT: Based on sales of over 5,000 hats in the first six months, the Museum anticipated income of $100,000 in the program's first year, from both its 10% royalty fee and direct sales through its gift shop and magazine. In addition to the monetary rewards, the hat project serves a second purpose: Tags on each hat focus on the museum's mission by telling the story behind the hats and the museum's expedition and research program. Convinced of the importance of the new licensing program, and based on the success of its initial product, the Museum has established a new department to focus specifically on licensing ventures. It also has moved into the development of other products with top manufacturers, including home furnishings and collectibles. One of the first results was the Museum's second major new product: fabrics inspired by objects in the collection, produced by Richloom Fabrics under a major licensing contract.

2

THE SIGN OF THE ARTIST:

Whimsical Touch

CHALLENGE: When you're a volunteer like Karen Goldstein, running an arts group's gift shop, you're always looking for the hot new item to sell. Seeking something special to herald her opera company's new season, Ms. Goldstein—a board member of the Arizona Opera League—remembered a wonderful poster that Arizona artist John Dawson had executed for the company's production of *Madama Butterfly*.

PLAN: Ms. Goldstein contacted the artist and Dawson, an opera lover himself, promised to come up with a design that would appeal to a broad audience. Injecting a nostalgic and whimsical note into his design, Dawson came up with a colorful poster showing various opera characters in costume with one notable addition: zany comedian Harpo Marx appearing in *A Night at the Opera*.

RESULT: The poster, copies of which sold for $25 each, was an immediate hit, enhanced by the personal involvement of the artist. Dawson made himself available for personal appearances at the gift shop and attended all three performances of each of the company's four operas that season, along with preview performances to inscribe buyers' posters personally. The autographed posters sold for $50-75 and the poster image was also turned into opera T-shirts and sweatshirts.

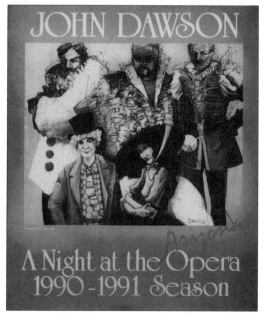

The Arizona Opera's offbeat season poster, created by artist John Dawson.

"Everyone loved the poster," recalled Goldstein, "and John Dawson's contribution of his time and his services really helped sales." The posters not only earned over $6,000 for the opera company, but gave it a good publicity boost as well.

3

MUCH ADOO ABOUT THE ZOO:

Waste Brings Big Bucks

CHALLENGE: Most cultural institutions are acquisitive by both need and nature. Whether on the trail of elusive funds, new subscribers, paintings for collections or names for their mailing lists, acquisition goes with the territory. Yet, there are some cultural groups—Seattle's Woodland Park Zoo among them—for which subtracting rather than adding is a major concern. Specifically, the Zoo was seeking a way to cut the considerable cost of disposing of some 500 tons of animal waste a year.

PLAN: Although the zoo had experimented with delivering its manure to nearby community gardens, public health concerns led it to look for a more permanent solution. Following a year of experimentation with composting, the zoo applied to the agency responsible for managing Seattle's solid waste—the city's Engineering Department—to fund a modest one-year pilot project that would blend the plentiful animal waste with straw bedding, grass, leaves and wood chips from the

Woodland Park Zoo is proud to provide Seattle area gardeners with Zoo Doo, a fine bulk compost.

The City of Seattle is dedicated to reduction, re-use and recycling of "waste" materials. Woodland Park Zoo supports this Commitment by offering Zoo Doo for sale to the public.

The Zoo Doo program of Seattle's Woodland Park Zoo.

Zoo's grounds into a new and needed product. The funded project, undertaken in conjunction with the city's Solid Waste Utility and Public Health Department, and led by a part-time coordinator armed with new brochures and an answering machine, resulted in Zoo Doo: a fine bulk compost to be offered for sale to local gardeners.

RESULT: Zoo Doo, recognized as the highest quality bulk compost available in the Seattle area, was an instant success with local gardeners, with product demand outstripping supply from the beginning. It now saves the Zoo about $40,000 annually in disposal fees (up from $7,000 the first year) while earning enough from sales (about $15,000 a year) to just about cover the cost of running the program. Not only has Zoo Doo become a popular product for Seattle's gardeners (who buy it in bulk at $16 a cubic yard—by appointment) but it's become a popular holiday gift item, with a small amount pre-bagged and sold at the end of the year as HoliDoo. Coordinated by a Parks and Recreation Department employee—known locally as Dr. Doo—the program has been promoted with a light touch, as evidenced by the "Zoo Doo Poopsheet" and Dr. Doo's phone number: 625-Poop. While saving and earning money at the same time, the program also has had a public relations and educational value for the zoo. The Garden and Compost Demonstration site at the Zoo's Family Farm, which houses the Zoo Doo project, attracts thousands of visitors annually, who learn about intensive gardening and small-scale composting.

4

WHAT A DIFFERENCE A BROCHURE MAKES:

Freshening Up

CHALLENGE: Since the 1970s, the New Orleans Opera Association has earned significant income every year by renting its production sets through its own scene shop, the H. Lloyd Hawkins Scenic Studio. But although sets offered were of top quality and sales were still relatively high in the early 90s—reaching just over $100,000—a ten percent revenue drop convinced the company that it was time to find a new way of selling its product. Perhaps, staff members thought, a more attractive brochure might help boost sales.

PLAN: The company completely revamped its brochure, substituting a new concept and design for the old foldover model. What emerged was a packet with pockets to hold separate glossy color pages for each opera offered. Each insert showed three or four sets from the featured opera, along with quotes from newspapers around the country on their design and elegance. A separate page listed all the operas and set designers, the year they were made and the number of trucks needed to transport them. Each time the company built or added a set to its inventory, it inserted into the brochure a new page with color photos and quotes. Packets are mailed every fall and spring to general, technical and artistic directors of opera companies in the U.S. and Canada.

RESULT: In the first year of the new approach, packets sent to 100 opera companies resulted in $156,000 in rentals, more than a 50% increase over the previous year. The next year, packets mailed to 230 companies resulted in record revenues of $216,000. The Opera attributes the revenue jump to the increased marketplace visibility the new packets have given the program.

Chapter Ten

Business Support

1

SELLING THE NEIGHBORHOOD:

Sponsoring Location

CHALLENGE: San Diego's Gaslamp Quarter Theatre Company needed a $100,000 donation to meet its matching-fund campaign goal.

PLAN: Because of its location in the city's downtown waterfront district, then being redeveloped, the theatre decided to focus its approach on a business tied to the area and interested in its development. The target was Stark Properties, constructing a high-rise luxury condominium around the corner—with 200 apartments selling for from $271,000 to $2.6 million. The theatre's four-page proposal pitched the importance of the district's amenities to potential apartment buyers by listing as one of the campaigns' key objectives, "the creation of a world-class waterfront district, known for its warmth, elegance, entertainment, extraordinary architecture, cultural richness, and *resounding success.*" The proposal—which asked for $100,000—focused on six evenings designed to give potential condominium buyers "a taste of city living at its finest," and offered a range of promotional tie-ins as well as one-year theatre subscriptions for condominium buyers. Each evening was to include a buffet dinner with live music and cocktails catered by an area restaurant at the condominium sales office, dessert and coffee at the condominium site and a red carpet walkway to the theatre for a Gaslamp Quarter performance.

RESULT: Two weeks after the proposal's submission, a Stark Properties executive launched the promotion with the presentation onstage of a $100,000 check to the theatre. In all, seven evenings—each attended by about 100 prospective apartment buyers—were held.

One Harbor Drive
and
The Gaslamp Quarter Theatre Company
cordially invite you to
"Full House Night"

ONE HARBOR DRIVE

A very special evening of sampling the delights of downtown living
Dinner begins at 5:30 PM
at Stark Properties, 205 G Street featuring
"A Taste of Gaslamp" fare

Followed by a visit to the site of One Harbor Drive luxury condominiums
and a performance of
"Cat on a Hot Tin Roof"
at The Hahn Cosmopolitan Theatre

GASLAMP
QUARTER
THEATRE
COMPANY

March 13, April 3 or April 16, 1992

Please reply to Jill at 232-9608. Reserve early. Space is very limited.

Flier for the Gaslamp Quarter Theatre Company's sponsorship program with a realty concern.

2

THAT EXTRA OUNCE:

Meeting Mutual Needs

CHALLENGE: The Arena Stage in Washington, D.C. wanted to promote its new day-of-performance, half-price HOTTIX program to audiences that had yet to discover the theatre. Remy Martin Cognac wanted to introduce potential new buyers to its product. Together, they were able to forge a creative partnership that more than met their respective hoped-for goals.

RESULT: Remy Martin agreed to sponsor the marketing of the HOTTIX program and underwrite all advertising, promotion, and direct mail costs—including mailing 30,000 program brochures to Arena's in-house list and purchased demographic lists. To give a real boost to the promotion, however, a special event was scheduled, with a hard-to-resist offer. To encourage an immediate response, Remy Martin offered to exchange all proofs-of-purchase of its Cognac during a designated month-long period for two complimentary tickets to "Remy Night at Arena Stage," an evening which included not only a performance of *A Chorus of Disapproval* but a gala celebration at a nearby restaurant afterwards. Remy Martin backed up the offer with in-store displays at over 100 Washington-area stores and full-page ads in the *Washington Post* and the *City Paper*.

RESULT: As a result of an overwhelming response—with more than 1,000 people taking advantage of the offer—Arena had to add two additional theatre evenings for the Cognac buyers. Remy Martin was so pleased with the successful introductory offer that, later that season, it again offered to exchange proofs-of-purchase for another Arena event. This time, however, audiences had to *buy* tickets for Arena Stage's production of the musical *On the Town*, for any night of their choice, in order to receive complimentary invitations to a gala party sponsored by Remy Martin. At the party—the nautical theme of which captured the spirit of the Arena production— guests were feted with food and drink, and received specially designed nautical T-shirts, compliments of Remy productions, since they provided an attention-getting launching pad for the HOTTIX program. Moreover, in addition to the promotional value, there were measurable results as well: Over half the respondents to the initial offer of Remy Night at Arena Stage had never attended an Arena performance before.

3

BUSINESS QUID PRO QUO:

Cooperative Project

CHALLENGE: The Cleveland Ballet sought to boost family ticket sales for its holiday *Nutcracker* performances, and to reach potential audiences not on its regular mailing list. BP Oil, a ballet-company sponsor, wanted to provide extra benefits at holiday time for its charge-card customers. A cooperative project, allowing both the dance company and the oil company to reach their respective objectives needed to be developed.

PLAN: David Oakland, general manager of the dance company, met with BP marketing executives and asked them what kind of program was best for them and their customers. When the executives said that, as corporate donors, they were interested in projects that would provide a measurable return to their customers and employees and which also would have a lasting positive impact on the nonprofit beneficiary, Oakland came up with a promotional concept: Instead of asking BP to pay for a mailing, the dance company would undertake its own special half-price ticket mailing to a list of BP credit-card customers, which the oil company would provide. To make sure that only potential new customers were on the list, the dance company would purge any duplicate names. An important aspect of the offer was that potential buyers, in addition to the savings on tickets, were given the option of paying by check or charging ticket purchases to their BP Oil Card, "allowing you extra time to pay."

RESULT: The dance company mailed 136,000 brochures to BP customers outside of the normal Cleveland Ballet ticket-buying area; the only seats offered were for performance days that, historically, had a poor purchase record. Within three weeks, the dance company received 8,700 new orders which, importantly, were all from new customers, and for seats that had never sold before. "The discount coupled with the payment option drove its success," said Oakland. With both parties pleased with the program's success, follow-up cooperative ventures were organized. In a unique linking, the Cleveland Ballet put together similar programs for other dance companies—the Pittsburgh Ballet Theatre, North Carolina Dance Theatre and Atlanta Ballet—in markets where BP had large customer bases. Building on its BP relationship, the following summer the Cleveland Ballet mailed a half-price weekend, three-performance subscription offer to 400,000 BP customers in the greater Cleveland area. Aimed at families again, the offer included the revolving payment option as well as an offer to add on a child's seat for only $10 more per performance.

"Our BP program worked for us for several reasons," claimed Oakland. "First, we had a large inventory of seats to sell. Second, there was a demand for the artistic product and price was a barrier. Third, the large number of potential ticket orders supported a $50,000 cost to the dance company, because even with a one-percent return, we knew that we would come out ahead—which we did. Unless an organization has the resources to get into direct mail, and at least one million dollars' worth of inventory for a product the public wants, it wouldn't pay for an arts group to undertake this kind of project."

4

HAVE ANOTHER BEER:

Replacing Departing Sponsor

CHALLENGE: The Fortune Theatre Company in Dunedin, New Zealand—which bills itself as the world's southernmost full-time professional theatre company—suffered a key loss when a corporate sponsor, Dominion Breweries, moved control of its local operation to another city and, in a change of policy, dropped its support of the theatre. With the lost-sponsorship revenue valued at nearly one-fourth of the company's total sponsorship income of $40,000, a replacement was clearly needed.

PLAN: When a key volunteer supporter of the Fortune, Crawford Brown, was appointed Master Brewer for another major New Zealand brewery—Speights—an opportunity presented itself. Brown indicated that the brewery might be interested in helping the company meet a long-time need—the purchase of a truck for use in touring and in carting theatre sets. Fortune's sponsorship proposal went right to the point: In return for paying off Fortune's entire bank loan over three years—to allow the theatre to purchase the truck without cost—Speights would have signage on the truck. Also, the bar at the Fortune Theatre would have Speights signage and would be stocked with Speights products.

RESULT: Only months after the sponsorship was arranged, the theatre's new truck (having first been inspected by Speights engineers) was out on the streets. As the new three-year relationship—valued at over $20,000—got under way, the theatre won still another benefit: Two of its upcoming productions were to have onstage products supplied by Speights without charge.

5

MATCHING IDENTITIES:

Identifying with Business Sponsor

CHALLENGE: When the London Mozart Players—the city's longest-established chamber orchestra—looks for corporate funding, it seeks companies with which it can match identities, either through its overall program or through special projects it wishes to develop. With this in mind, the orchestra set out to find a sponsor for its informal, family-oriented, Sunday-afternoon concert series at London's Barbican Centre, featuring new conductors and new soloists and including opportunities for the audience to meet the musicians and talk to them.

PLAN: Late afternoons are tea time in England, and what better match could be made than a tea-concert series, featuring tasting intervals of different herbal teas, with complimentary biscuits, sponsored by a well-known tea company? The London Mozart Players found the London Herb & Spice Company a logical and willing sponsor, and the company underwrote the series for two years, providing tea, biscuits and sample gifts along with the funding. To emphasize the tea connection, individual concerts had such titles as the "Peppermint Tea Concert," the "Orange Dazzler Tea Concert," the "Cherry Pickers Punch Tea Concert," the "Strawberry Fair Tea

The London Mozart Players' flier for its tea concert series sponsored by London Herb & Spice Company.

Concert." At the suggestion of the Players, which wanted promotional materials that were not only attractive but that would enable concertgoers to identify the tea in shops, the tea company commissioned an artist to design the posters and leaflets based on the packaging design.

RESULT: Promoted with the tag line, "Take Tea With the LMP," the concerts were sellouts and introduced a new audience to classical music. The LMP also realized a significant £59,000 from the sponsorships. The sponsor not only achieved its marketing objectives, but won an award from the Association for Business Sponsorship of the Arts. When it bowed out after several years, the series continued with a new sponsor, Ridgways Organically Grown Tea.

6

INVOLVING THE SPONSOR:

Sponsor Reaches Out

CHALLENGE: The New Jersey Performing Arts Center, a $150-million cultural center in Newark that was still several years away from being built, had been developing programs and services far in advance of its opening to help attract audiences and support. One such program was its sponsorship of a five-week residency by Jacques D'Amboise's National Dance Institute in local schools, set to culminate in one public and several more private performances of the Institute's well-known *Fat City* in Newark's Symphony Hall. To carry out the activity—a key one because of its visibility and community involvement—the Center needed $100,000, with a corporation the most logical underwriting target.

PLAN: The Center's development team focused on large corporate donors in the state which already had made major contributions. One such company, the A&P supermarket chain, was not only headquartered in nearby Montvale, New Jersey, but also was personally involved in the Center's future through its chairman, who volunteered his help on several occasions. As one of the state's top employers, and a company with a strong stake in developing good customer relations, A&P seemed a good prospect. The Center also recognized that—precisely because of its visibility in the state—A&P could play an even larger role in the program, by getting other companies involved.

After A&P agreed to the $100,000 sponsorship, which paid for the performances and the residency, it turned around and used its involvement to attract even more support, asking its customers and suppliers to attend a post-performance dinner, with

A&P suggesting sponsorship packages available to them at $10,000 or $25,000. Less expensive packages for smaller venders were sold as well and companies also were asked to buy advertising space in a commemorative program.

RESULT: Thanks to the leverage wielded by A&P, 320 people attended the dinner, including representatives of many companies never before involved with the Center. (Some 60 corporations were added to the Center's database of potential corporate sponsors.) The money received was equally good. In addition to A&P's $100,000 sponsorship, the Center netted over $350,000 from the event.

7

BACK TO BUSINESS:

Reviving Old Proposal with New Twist

CHALLENGE: Kay Kjelland, executive director, of the North Valley Arts Council in Grand Forks, North Dakota, was eager to participate in the first National Arts and Humanities Month. What's more, she had an idea that—with the involvement of local business—could really promote arts and humanities activity in the area: have a local grocery chain list all area arts and humanities organizations on its shopping bags. When she broached the subject with the management of Hugo's, a chain with seven stores in North Dakota and nearby Minnesota, she found she was too late to have the bags ready in time. Undaunted, she decided she would go back to Hugo's the following year with a proposal it couldn't ignore.

PLAN: The next year, Kjelland visited Curt Magnuson, the head of Hugo's and the founder's son, with a written proposal that stressed the dedication of the area's cultural community. If Hugo's would feature arts and humanities groups on all its shopping bags during the second National Arts and Humanities Month, she would give Hugo's the inside front cover of the Arts Council magazine for its own use. Hugo's agreed. Kjelland next approached the First National Bank in Grand Forks for a donation which would be used to promote the month: when the bank indicated that it had used up all of that year's funds for contributions months earlier, she thought of the Hugo's promotion and offered the inside *back* cover to the bank it if would enclose the same list of arts and humanities groups with its bank statements. It too agreed.

RESULT: For one month, thousands of Hugo's shopping bags—used by all its stores—listed all of the region's local cultural organizations along with the slogan, "Take a Bite Out of Life. Enjoy Local Arts and Culture." Also included on the bag was the logo and phone number of the Arts Council. During the same period, some 12,000 statements were mailed by the bank to its customers in the greater Grand Forks area—with the same listing, phone number and Arts Council logo, but with a slightly different message: "Arts and Culture. You Can Bank On It." Kjelland was very pleased with the results. "We had tremendous exposure and we received phone calls from people who saw our phone number listed. What was most important about the promotion was that we were able to reach many, many people whom we don't ordinarily reach."

8

BAGGING THE ARTS:

Promotional Shopping Bags

CHALLENGE: As the Los Angeles Music Center Opera was preparing for its first season, staff and volunteers were looking for new and imaginative ways to promote it.

PLAN: A board member of the Los Angeles Opera League—the wife of an executive at Trader Joe's, a chain of specialty food stores in California and Arizona—had an idea that would market the opera company to millions of people. With Placido Domingo doing *Otello* as the opera's premiere performance, why not promote the performance and the company on the face of Trader Joe's shopping bags?

RESULT: The shopping bags became such an immediate hit that shoppers started collecting them. They were so popular, in fact, that other arts groups started knocking on Trader Joe's doors asking if they might get "bagging" rights as well. Throughout the duration of the program, Trader Joe's shopping bags promoted five or six arts groups of every type each year. After groups won the go-ahead, they prepared the ad and gave Trader Joe's the camera-ready art and copy. Trader Joe's then took over the manufacturing and distribution of an estimated million bags a month for its sixty-two stores. Often, the beneficiaries found special uses for the bags: the Los Angeles County High School for the Arts, for example, had a bag design contest among its students; later, when the bags were available, it gave them away as promotional items during a major fund drive.

A Trader Joe's shopping bag promoting local arts programs.

9

ANNIVERSARY WALTZ:

Linking Anniversaries

CHALLENGE: When an arts institution celebrates a significant anniversary, there's more at stake than good wishes and congratulations. As many groups have discovered, anniversaries provide unique marketing and fund-raising opportunities. With its seventy-fifth anniversary on the horizon, the Cleveland Play House was looking for such an opportunity when one presented itself at its doorstep: Through an interesting coincidence, a leading Cleveland law firm, Baker & Hostetler, also was celebrating its seventy-fifth anniversary and wanted to do something special to commemorate the date. After considering several options, the firm's partners decided that local arts groups, battered by cutbacks in government funding, needed all the help they could get. With the aid of a public-relations agency, several key Cleveland arts organizations were identified as possible recipients and asked to submit broad proposals to an unnamed "Cleveland service firm" that wanted to support the arts. The Cleveland Play House, which based its general proposal around its anniversary, was one of two finalists selected to make an on-target proposal for a partnership with the by-now identified law firm.

PLAN: Based on a meeting with several Baker & Hostetler partners, the Play House's development director submitted a plan that linked the firm to the theatre in an anniversary-year partnership. The theatre proposed promoting the partnership in all its materials, including: full-page ads in each of the season's production program books; title page recognition in the program; a full-page dedication in the theatre's commemorative anniversary book; and banners up and down Euclid Avenue. The law firm would receive performance tickets and—of key significance—they would have use of the Play House site for an anniversary cocktail reception and dinner party. (When the anniversary party was held several months later, the law firm was feted with an original forty-five minute theatre piece, "The Law Review," developed and presented by the Lab Company, an ensemble of MFA acting candidates from Ohio University and nationally selected directing and playwriting fellows who intern for an entire season at the theatre.) It didn't hurt the Play House cause when the law firm went back into its records and discovered that, many years earlier, a Baker & Hostetler partner had been president of the Cleveland Play House.

RESULT: Baker & Hostetler made a $250,000 donation to the Cleveland Play House—the largest grant in the theatre's history—to sponsor the theatre's anniversary season. It also recognized other local arts groups by announcing a program to donate $50,000 to one arts group a year for the following five years. Buoyed by the Baker & Hostetler grant and attendant publicity, the Cleveland Play House increased overall funding that season by 38% (21% without the law-firm gift). The most significant gain was in individual giving, with donations up 24% from $550,000 to $702,000.

10

MUG SHOT:

Brand Recognition for Sponsor

CHALLENGE: Very Special Arts has very special needs which allies its marketing and development. Because its program is designed to enrich the lives of people with disabilities by involving them in the arts, it is constantly looking for ways to develop funded programs that build awareness of the organization and its activities, and to promote the talents of disabled artists. One of its most successful approaches is to find a corporate sponsor which not only has the resources to support VSA and the means to disseminate its message, but specific business objectives which can be met through a partnership with VSA.

PLAN: VSA targeted the Maxwell House Coffee Company, a division of Kraft General Foods, which—in a highly competitive field—is always looking for ways to differentiate its brands from other coffees. The plan VSA presented to Maxwell House was to have an artist with a disability decorate coffee cans, and VSA stressed the fact that the promotion would not only help create positive consumer attitudes toward the Maxwell House brand, but that it would add value to the consumer purchase, since the coffee tins created would become collectibles. A funding feature was added to the proposal, with the suggestion that the coffee company sell mugs featuring the same artist's work, with VSA collecting a portion of the earnings from the sales.

RESULT: Maxwell House distributed 3.1-million coffee cans featuring artwork created by Randy Souders, an artist with a disability and a VSA board member. The VSA name and logo was included on the face of each can, with special promotional inserts inside describing VSA's concept and program. Maxwell House also promoted a special offer: for $5 consumers could order designer mugs featuring Souders' work. Not only did VSA benefit tremendously through exposure to millions of consumer, but it made money also. With the $1 it received from the sale of each mug, VSA raised an estimated $25,000. Important to VSA also was the fact that Maxwell House benefited from the consumer promotion as well, winning positive feedback from consumers and the retail trade.

11

HITTING THE HIGH C's:

Unique Facilities

CHALLENGE: With its twentieth birthday approaching, the Sydney Opera House recognized that its unique waterfront setting and its renown as Australia's prime tourist attraction could make the occasion a powerful vehicle for reaching potential sponsors. Seeking a program that would capture younger and larger audiences, the Opera House marketing staff eyed Sydney Harbor and its Aquashell—a floating stage leased by Prudential Insurance.

PLAN: The Opera House approached Prudential with an interesting sponsorship proposition which the company bought—that it sponsor a free concert by the Sydney Opera House Orchestra and donate use of the Aquashell. Promoted widely, "The Sydney Opera House Goes to Sea on the Prudential Aquashell" attracted an audience of about 10,000 people who, in a park-like setting adjacent to the Opera House, which served as a backdrop, heard the "floating orchestra" perform such appropriate classics as *Swan Lake* and Handel's *Water Music*. The spectacular finale featured a performance of the *Royal Fireworks Suite* accompanied by a fireworks display. A

Prudential flier promoting the event indicated how pleased it was with its involvement. "Without our floating stage," it read, "tonight's free concert would be Handel's Underwater Music."

RESULT: Not only did the Opera House have a memorable birthday celebration—not to mention a cash donation of $50,000 from Prudential—but it also saw the beginning of a new water-based relationship with its sponsor. Delighted with the recognition it had won, Prudential provided the Aquashell again the following year and increased its cash donation to $75,000 for what was termed "an even more gala event," a "Strauss Beneath the Stars" concert. Not incidentally, the same Opera House birthday was used to attract sponsorship for another large, free, community-oriented event. On the evening of "Open Day"—when the Opera House as a climax to its anniversary celebration opened its doors to the public—Coca-Cola Amatil sponsored a free evening concert by Wendy Matthews in the Opera House Forecourt. Open Day drew 100,000 visitors, and 60,000 remained for the nationally televised evening concert. In addition to attracting the young audience it was aiming for, the Opera House benefited from extensive national publicity and goodwill—and picked up a $100,000 sponsorship in the process.

12

LOCAL BUSINESS PARTNERSHIPS:

Ongoing Aid

CHALLENGE: The Plainsboro Cultural Affairs Committee, a group of arts, business and community leaders appointed by the Township of Plainsboro, New Jersey was seeking an effective way to involve local business in supporting community arts activity on an ongoing basis.

PLAN: The Committee organized a "Plainsboro Arts Partnership," a public/private venture to involve local businesses in a continuing relationship with the arts community—one that would provide benefits on both sides of the equation, would focus specifically on the Plainsboro area, and would involve company employees directly in the resulting programs as both planners and participants. The Partnership's written agreement, signed by all business members, asks them to make three commitments: to find or organize a consortium to manage a cultural event; to offer the event to those who live or work in Plainsboro; and to offer the event at a location in Plainsboro. It is also hoped that the events will provide opportunities for press coverage and image enhancement. The Partnership is promoted annually at an informal reception for current and prospective participants, with each attendee receiving a special brochure that provides program background, goals and benefits, reviews past sponsorships and offers one-page descriptions of programs available for sponsorship.

RESULT: The Partnership has grown every year since its inception. In its first four years, local businesses—from large international companies to small retail establishments and professional offices—sponsored over 100 cultural events, with support both in cash donations and in-kind services ranging from a few hundred dollars to as much as $15,000. Sponsored programs have included everything from youth orchestra concerts to jazz lecture series to outdoor band concerts and fireworks. As a result of the Partnership success, an informal resource network has emerged which provides new sponsors with help on sites, publicity and operations.

A Plainsboro Arts Partnership Agreement.

Chapter Eleven

The Tourist Trade

1

ONSTAGE HOSPITALITY:

Involving Local Industry

CHALLENGE: Arts spaces need the involvement and support of local hotels, restaurants and limousine services, which can play critical roles in promoting arts events to their patrons. But as Jimmy Hilburger, director of marketing for Michigan State University's Wharton Center for Performing Arts recognized, the hospitality industry in his community often took its own need for top-quality cultural events for granted. Clearly, to capitalize on a mutual dependency and the advantages that a smooth working relationship could bring to both parties, hospitality industry leaders had to be aware of upcoming events at the Center, and learn how they could utilize those events to their best advantage.

PLAN: Using a promotional campaign built around the slogan, "Spend a Night on the Town," Hilburger and other staff members set out to plan a special onstage party for key hospitality industry officials at the Wharton Center a month before the season's start. The state's hotel/restaurant association membership roster and area phone books were combed to develop a guest list that included all hotels and private clubs, limousine services and every restaurant with a liquor license within a thirty-mile radius of the East Lansing, Michigan arts center. Hilburger added advertising and news department representatives of area newspapers, radio and television stations to the list to give media people the opportunity to preview the Wharton Center season and to allow sales reps to mingle with potential advertisers who, according to Hilburger, "might want to ride the wave of Wharton Center's marketing campaign." The party itself, which attracted more than seventy-five people, was a deluxe event, with food stations serving such delicacies as pork flambé, caviar and vodka (donated, along with other alcoholic beverages, by two radio stations) set in sterling silver ice buckets. Guests mingled onstage—looking out to the audience area where life-size blow-ups of performers for the upcoming season had been placed—before moving to individual music stands equipped with lights and press kits. For the program portion, Hilburger mounted the conductor's podium to discuss the season and the kind of audience each event might draw, and to pinpoint the benefits of a partnership with the arts center. He discussed, for example, how special meals could be offered to relate to the range of international attractions at the Center. He also pointed out two local restaurants that already benefited by buying 40 to 100 tickets at group discount rates and then sold theatre/dinner packages, including buses to and from the Center, with post-performance drinks and dessert at the restaurant.

RESULT: The evening was so successful that it became an annual event. Restaurants and hotels began making their own table tents, promoting both Wharton Center events and their own theatre/dinner packages, and featuring Wharton Center posters on their bulletin boards and in their display cases. New group restaurant and hotel packages were introduced, and one hotel even promoted a weekend getaway package, with theatre tickets aimed specifically at local residents. Perhaps most significant from the perspective of Hilburger, who has since moved to another arts center, was the event's role in helping turn introductions into long-term, profitable partnerships.

2

JAM SESSION:

Promotable Names

CHALLENGE: Following three years of informal networking, the managers of Townsville, Australia's ten professional arts groups, were about to take a major step forward. Incorporated as the Townsville Professional Arts Working Group (PAWG), the managers had submitted a successful application to the Australia Council for a new pilot project: development of Australia's first arts-marketing consortium. Thanks to a A $40,000 grant from the Council, $8,500 in contributions from PAWG constituents and sponsorship for area business groups—including a furnished office and equipment—PAWG hired a top professional marketing director and set out to develop a marketing program that would attract attention and encourage participation in the arts.

PLAN: Because there was a need to arouse and involve the community, eye-catching graphics and attention-getting concepts were integral to the overall plan. Activities over the first nine months included: mailing of a questionnaire to area households by the regional electric authority, resulting in a categorized consumer mailing list; an arts calendar appearing weekly in the regional *Townsville Bulletin*; a new tourism brochure promoting local art galleries and museums; a two-day cultural tourism seminar; and the commissioning of specially designed boards—each featuring a single descriptive work, such as theatre or dance, and an interesting graphic—to be used as backdrops for promotional and informational displays. Equally important to the entire promotional effort was the decision to substitute a catchy and snappy name for PAWG. When Joint Arts Marketing for Townsville or "JAM for T" was adopted as a name early in the program, it provided an exciting new look and new sound to the project as well as a useful marketing tool. The result was not only the use of a new "JAM for T" logo on all program materials but the use of "JAM" in a range of ways, including the distribution of small jars of jam provided by an Australian firm, O'Brien Cherry Berry Jams. In addition to the logo, the jars of jam included a small wraparound promoting the arts of Townsville.

RESULT: The campaign, which had a very successful first year, alerted both residents and tourists to the lively cultural life in Townsville. Although the project lost its Council funding after a year due to government cutbacks—resulting in the departure of its paid marketing director—the participating arts groups have since kept the project going on the proverbial shoestring, with volunteer help and the use of a coordinator for five hours a week.

$$\overline{\underline{3}}$$

Putting Art on the Map:

Arts/Tourism Trail

CHALLENGE: Among the goals outlined by the Nelson Bays Arts Marketing Network in New Zealand were the development of partnerships between the area's arts community and local businesses, and the initiation of projects that would benefit the arts sector, help it market its work collectively and ensure the Network's financial stability. Since Nelson was a tourist area noted for its scenic beauty, its excellent climate and its many artists and craftspersons, Network leaders recognized that both artists and tourism-oriented businesses might be attracted to a cooperative promotion that used the arts to attract and serve tourists.

PLAN: An idea came to trustee Anne Rush and executive Mary Jensen as they were winding their way between the studios of several artists: a guidebook that would not only identify local art trails and link them to vineyards and restaurants, but would provide heritage, environmental and tourism information. Only a month later, Network leaders were putting together an initial plan for the book. After seeking advice from a local publisher and receiving a range of quotes, a $50,000 budget was established for the printing of a 100-page full-color book. As determined by a business advisory group, income to produce the book would come from fees for short, half, and full-page listings for artists—100 half-pages would bring in about $25,000—and from advertising space sold to the hospitality industry. Network leaders held meetings with trustees and others to refine the project and, despite some dire warnings that the book could not be produced in the ten months scheduled, the Network sent out 300 invitations to the visual-arts community for presentations on the book and other planned Network initiatives. Three consecutive nights attracted 140 artists and craftspersons, during which marketing strategy for the book was outlined, visuals of the proposed cover and pages were displayed, and forms for attendees to complete were distributed. Within a month, after seventy-one artists had indicated they would take space in the book at an average of $250 a listing, a decision was made to move ahead. During the next two months, the pace increased, with

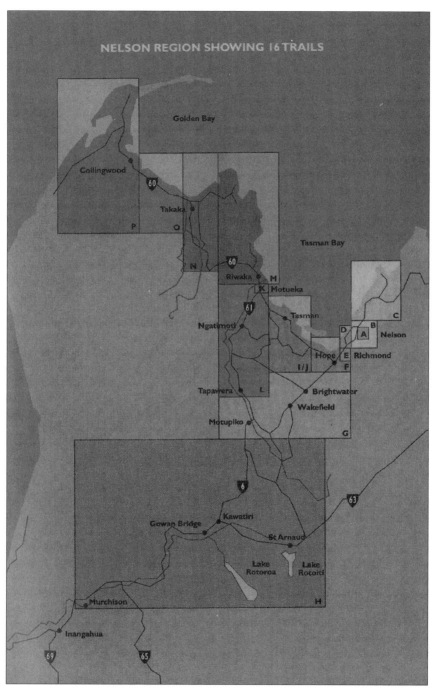

The Nelson Bays Arts Marketing Network's book, the *Nelson Regional Guide: Art in Its Own Place.*

newsletters sent to all 300 invitees, listings entered into a computer, fees collected and an advertising sales campaign aimed at the hospitality industry launched by a trustee. Production work began, with a cartographer-turned-potter commissioned to draw up artist trails, and a photographer hired and volunteer writers recruited to prepare copy on the area's history and attractions. Listings were finalized with commitments from 130 artists and thirty-two hospitality stops (which paid more for their listings than the artists). Over $26,000 had been raised, with $5,000 more coming in the form of a grant from the Lottery Environment and Heritage Fund. With printing paid for by fees, the book was resized to 136 pages, and a cashflow forecast was completed for an initial 5,000-copy print run. The break-even point was pegged at 3,000 copies sold over two years at $16.95 retail, which seemed well within reach.

RESULT: Confounding the skeptics, the *Nelson Regional Guide: Art in Its Own Place* was introduced locally—slightly ahead of schedule—as part of a week-long promotion, "Art in its Own Place—in Your Place." The handsome book, with maps and listings of sixteen different trails, information pages, and full-page photos had been completed in only nine months. It was an instant hit, with more than 1,000 copies sold in the first week.

4

ROOM AND BARD:

Partnership with Hotels

CHALLENGE: As tourism becomes increasingly important, many arts groups have developed cooperative programs with local hotels, linking room bookings with performance or exhibition tickets. The Alabama Shakespeare Festival in Montgomery has long recognized the tourist market's significance, offering special packages to patrons. Although hotel packages generated more than $96,000 in yearly revenue, ASF decided that the program's potential would be enhanced and its efficiency (and profitability) increased through exclusive partnership with a single major hotel chain.

PLAN: With three quality hotels located less than a mile from the Festival, Marriott seemed a perfect partner. A proposal to Marriott showed how the participating hotels would benefit from ASF's operation, its experienced sales and box office staffs, its printed materials and its direct mail and advertising programs, and how a partnership could boost hotel room rentals on weekends, traditionally a slow period for hotels. Marriott was interested, so ASF produced a brochure focusing on the "Simple as 1, 2, 3" link between the Festival and the hotels. With one call to the theatre's 800-number, patrons could order two tickets for two plays and have three choices of accommodations at great discounts. "Stay overnight at Marriott for as low as $111 per couple," the brochure stated, "and see two plays from ASF's 22nd season."

RESULT: The exclusive hotel relationship boosted sales and income for both theatre and hotels. With revenues near $200,000 that year the hotels realized close to $100,000 and the theatre $92,000, a figure that increased to $97,000 the next year, despite the fact that the theatre had not increased ticket prices in the hotel package for three years. However, since all three Marriott Hotels paid an additional fee for the exclusive arrangement, the theatre revenue actually increased substantially. Things looked even better the following year when prices were increased and the Festival and the three Marriott Hotels renewed their exclusive arrangement.

5

THE ULTIMATE ARTS EXPERIENCE:

City Plan

CHALLENGE: With its near-perfect climate and proximity to Mexico, San Diego draws large numbers of tourists each year. The city's Arts & Culture Commission, however, recognized that there was an opportunity to attract even more people if it could convince San Diego's Convention and Visitors Bureau that the city's thriving arts industry should be made a more integral part of the city's overall tourism promotion program.

PLAN: With impetus from the Culture Commission, a Joint Research Committee (JRC), with membership from the staff and board of both the Commission and the Convention and Visitors Bureau, was established with a specific goal—to determine how to promote cultural tourism more effectively. Over several months, the Committee reviewed each agency's then-current cultural tourism promotion programs and gathered data on the promotion of cultural tourism in eight cities throughout the country, comparing them on the basis of ten different criteria. Out of a matrix developed from the material it gathered, the JRC developed an inventory of ideas that it put together into a specific plan of action. The three-year plan was adopted by the boards of both the Cultural Commission and the Convention and Visitors Bureau and became part of San Diego's overall Economic Development Strategic Plan.

RESULT: An immediate benefit of the program was the establishment of a strong and close working relationship between the Convention Bureau and the Culture Commission. Within a year after adoption of the plan, 100,000 copies of a new, multicolor *Ultimate Arts and Culture Guide to San Diego* were published and distributed through the city's Visitors Center and the Bureau. Also, as the promotion of cultural activities became a key component of the Bureau's marketing effort, photos and copy on local arts program were featured more than ever in the *Official Visitors Guide* and other promotional materials. While not every recommendation in the plan was implemented, a start was made on several key efforts, including training hotel personnel to learn about arts programs and organizations in San Diego, and the development of new partnerships between major sporting-events presenters and the arts.

6

WOOING THE TOURISTS:

Investing in Promotion

CHALLENGE: The Aspen Music Festival, a long-time summer attraction in Aspen, Colorado wanted to expand its audience by attracting more tourists, but the Festival didn't have sufficient resources to do a first-class promotional campaign on its own.

PLAN: Because Aspen tourism is greatest during the winter ski season, the Festival reasoned that top local hotels would be as interested as it was in boosting summer visits. The Festival suggested to several hotels that they pool resources and develop a "Summer in Aspen" promotion during the winter aimed at travel agents and travel writers. The result was a series of evening receptions co-sponsored by the Festival, Aspen hotels, and an airline—which contributes travel for participating sponsors—featuring a brief performance by a Festival artist, a short video on Aspen in summer and informal meetings by hotel and Festival representatives with the attendees. Presented first in Los Angeles, San Francisco and San Diego, receptions also are now held in New York and Chicago. The Festival contributes $5,000 and other sponsors contribute $2,000 each.

RESULT: The program has been successful since its inception, at a fraction of what advertising and direct mail would cost. The number of out-of-state summer visitors to Aspen and the Festival has grown. Festival attendees from California alone have jumped from 15% of the total audience to 22%.

INDEX

INDEX

INDEX

INDEX